ROUGH GUIDES WALKS & TOURS
MADRID

YOUR TAILOR-MADE TRIP
STARTS HERE

Tailor-made trips and unique adventures crafted by local experts

Rough Guides has been inspiring travellers with lively and thought-provoking guidebooks for more than 35 years. Now we're linking you up with selected local experts to craft your dream trip. They will put together your perfect itinerary and book it at local rates.

Don't follow the crowd – find your own path.

HOW ROUGHGUIDES.COM/TRIPS WORKS

STEP 1

Pick your dream destination, tell us what you want and submit an enquiry.

STEP 2

Fill in a short form to tell your local expert about your dream trip and preferences.

STEP 3

Our local expert will craft your tailor-made itinerary. You'll be able to tweak and refine it until you're completely satisfied.

STEP 4

Book online with ease, pack your bags and enjoy the trip! Our local expert will be on hand 24/7 while you're on the road.

BENEFITS OF PLANNING AND BOOKING AT ROUGHGUIDES.COM/TRIPS

PLAN YOUR ADVENTURE WITH LOCAL EXPERTS

Rough Guides' English-speaking local experts are hand-picked, based on their experience in the travel industry and their impeccable standards of customer service.

SAVE TIME AND GET ACCESS TO LOCAL KNOWLEDGE

When a local expert plans your trip, you save time and money when you book, even during high season. You won't be charged for using a credit card either.

MAKE TRAVEL A BREEZE: BOOK WITH PEACE OF MIND

Enjoy stress-free travel when you use Rough Guides' secure online booking platform. All bookings come with a money-back guarantee.

WHAT DO OTHER TRAVELLERS THINK ABOUT ROUGH GUIDES TRIPS?

Trip to Spain

This Spain tour company did a fantastic job to make our dream trip perfect. We gave them our travel budget, told them where we would like to go, and they did all of the planning. Our drivers and tour guides were always on time and very knowledgable. The hotel accommodations were better than we would have found on our own. Only one time did we end up in a location that we had not intended to be in. We called the 24 hour phone number, and they immediately fixed the situation.

Don A, USA ★★★★★

Trip to Morocco

Our trip was fantastic! Transportation, accommodations, guides – all were well chosen! The hotels were well situated, well appointed and had helpful, friendly staff. All of the guides we had were very knowledgeable, patient, and flexible with our varied interests in the different sites. We particularly enjoyed the side trip to Tangier! Well done! The itinerary you arranged for us allowed maximum coverage of the country with time in each city for seeing the important places.

Sharon, USA ★★★★★

CONTENTS

Introduction

Trip plans

Directory

Architecture
Trace Madrid's history from the Habsburg buildings around the Plaza Mayor (walks 2 and 3) to the flamboyant style of the early twentieth-century on the Gran Vía (walk 1) and the modern Paseo de la Castellana (tour 12).

Best walks & tours for...

Art buffs
As well as the Thyssen-Bornemisza (walk 4) Prado and Reina Sofía museums (walk 5), don't miss the Real Academia de Bellas Artes de San Fernando (walk 1) and the Lázaro Galdiano and Sorolla museums (tour 12).

Families
Kids love the Natural Sciences museum and the Real Madrid stadium tour (tour 12), as well as the Teleférico cable car, the zoo and the Parque de Atracciones funfair in the Casa de Campo (walk 10).

Foodies
Sample local delicacies and Spanish wines at the Mercado de San Miguel gourmet market, then eat at a traditional restaurant with a wood-fired oven or do a tapas crawl on Cava Baja (all walk 2).

Night owls

There are night spots to suit all tastes in the Malasaña and Chueca neighbourhoods (walk 9), as well as in the streets around Plaza de Santa Ana (walk 7).

Romance

Make a special memory by watching the sunset at the Templo de Debod (walk 10) or from a terrace table at Las Vistillas (walk 3). Taking out a rowing boat in the Retiro Park can be pretty romantic too (walk 6).

Views

Take in the panoramic views from CentroCentro or the roof terrace at the Círculo de Bellas Artes (both walk 1). Get even higher up at the Faro observation tower in Moncloa (walk 11).

Back to nature

Breathe some fresh air in one of Madrid's green spaces. Stroll around the Retiro (walk 6) or the Botanical Garden (walk 5) and explore the Parque del Oeste (walk 10) and the Casa de Campo (walk 11).

INTRODUCTION

An introduction to Madrid and what makes it special, what not to miss and what to do when you're there.

Discover Madrid

Madrid is one of those places that just make people smile. With world-class museums, buzzing nightlife and a dynamic gastronomic scene, a visit to Spain's capital is sure to lift anyone's spirits.

Ask *madrileños* (Madrilenians) what they love most about their city and watch their eyes shine as they rave about the light and the vibrant atmosphere. Standing at an altitude of 667 metres (2,155ft), Madrid is the highest major capital city in Europe, which may account for the dazzling light and the clear blue skies, but it is the people themselves who create the exhilarating energy that all visitors notice as soon as they arrive.

You could spend weeks in Madrid just visiting the top museums, such as the Prado, Thyssen-Bornemisza and Reina Sofía, but allow plenty of time for just drifting around the tapas bars too, which counts as a cultural experience in its own right in Madrid. This is a city where the best-laid plans are likely to be forgotten soon after the first cold beer at a pavement terrace.

Despite the severe economic problems that Spain has gone through since 2008 and despite COVID, the centre of Madrid has undergone a startling transformation. Major urban renewal projects have completely changed Plaza Puerta del Sol, Plaza de España and Gran Via, all rebuilt to make them more pedestrian and bike-friendly. New shops, galleries and bars have popped up everywhere in previously dilapidated downtown areas. Look up, however, and you'll invariably still see someone in their dressing-gown, quietly taking in the scene from a wrought-iron balcony while watering their plants.

Geography and layout

Even though Madrid is a big capital city, it is surprisingly accessible with a compact central core. Wherever you stay, you can usually walk to the major museums and will often come across a lesser-known collection or gallery just around the corner – and there is nearly always an appealing tapas bar nearby too.

While it is by far the biggest city in Spain, most of the areas of interest to the visitor are concentrated around the city's core of the Puerta del Sol and are walkable for averagely-active people. Most of the routes in this book are less than five kilometres (3 miles), although striding around Madrid's many museums means you might cover a much greater distance.

If you follow walk 1 on arrival, walking from the Puerta del Sol to the

Sunrise over the city

Gran Vía, you will get a good idea of the layout of the city. The oldest part of town, Madrid de los Austrias (see walk 2), fans out west of the Puerta del Sol, around the Plaza Mayor. To the east is the characterful Barrio de la Letras around Plaza de Santa Ana (see walk 7), where many writers of the Golden Age lived. Now it is full of cafés and tapas bars. Immediately east of this area is the Paseo del Prado (see walks 4 and 5), the grand boulevard that was developed in the eighteenth century. Art lovers will be spending a lot of time walking up and down this stretch as they visit the three most important museums.

North of the Gran Vía, the narrow streets of Chueca, Malasaña and Conde Duque neighbourhoods have a lively vibe with lots of cafés and interesting little shops. To get an idea of how the city has expanded, take a trip up the Paseo de la Castellana, veering off to the east into the large Salamanca district to find the city's best boutiques.

History

Compared to other European cities, Madrid is a young capital. Arab groups from North Africa established a fortress in the ninth century, but Madrid only really got going when Felipe II chose it to be his capital in 1561 – moving the court from Toledo – because it was in a strategic position in the centre of Spain and the surrounding countryside was good for hunting.

While being named capital brought great wealth, it was helped enormously by this being Spain's Golden Age, with riches pouring in from the New World. This also led to the emergence of the first theatres and a lively cultural scene. The Bourbon monarch Carlos III implemented far-reaching urban developments, which included the transformation of the Paseo del Prado into an elegant boulevard lined with educational institutions. One of these was a vast building that was intended to be devoted to natural sciences but instead became the Prado art museum.

Upheavals in the nineteenth century culminated with the Spanish-American war of 1898, when Spain lost its last colonies of Cuba, Puerto Rico and the Philippines. This event had a profound effect on the mood of the nation and led to the creation of the intellectual movement known as the Generation of '98.

The twentieth century brought the devastating Civil War from 1936 to 1939, followed by the dictatorship of General Franco, which lasted until his death in 1975. The freedom brought by his death in 1975 led to the explosion of creativity known as *la movida madrileña*, with filmmaker Pedro Almodóvar as its figurehead.

King Juan Carlos I, who had reigned since 1975 following the death of Franco, abdicated in 2014, allowing his son to become king as Felipe VI at the age of 46. Perceived to be more in touch

Busy calle Preciados

Don't leave Madrid without...

Doing a tapas crawl. Some of the best food in the city comes in bite-sized portions. Drift from traditional tiled bars that have been going for a century or more to the sleek gastrobars where top chefs offer their creative cuisine in miniature form. See page 17.

Trying churros and chocolate. Eating churro fritters with a cup of gloopy hot chocolate in a traditional café is one of Madrid's most beloved customs. Although this calorific combo is most typical for breakfast, it goes down particularly well in the early hours after a night on the tiles. See page 40.

Walking around Madrid de los Austrias. Soak up the atmosphere of old Madrid by exploring the area around the Plaza Mayor, where the slate spires of the Habsburg period rise into the sky. At ground level, traditional taverns line the narrow streets. See page 32.

Visiting the museums on the Paseo del Arte. The Prado, Thyssen-Bornemisza, Reina Sofía and CaixaForum museums make this short stretch one of the best concentrations of art in the world. See the El Greco, Velázquez and Goya paintings at the Prado and Picasso's Guernica at the Reina

Sofía. See pages 48 and 52.

Drinking vermouth. Having a vermouth with a tapa at about 1pm is a favourite Madrid custom. Pop into the Mercado de San Miguel or one of the bars on and around the Plaza Mayor or down the road on Cava Baja. See page 33.

Shopping on calle Fuencarral. For a cool shopping vibe, join the throng strolling up the pedestrianised calle Fuencarral from the Gran Vía, where the boutiques alternate with hip cafés and bars. See page 21.

Browsing at the Rastro market on a Sunday morning. Hunt for a bargain at the sprawling flea market that spills down the hills below the Plaza Mayor on Sunday mornings. It is as much a social as a shopping expedition, with raucous tapas bars hidden behind the hundreds of stalls. See page 62.

Sauntering along the Gran Vía. Cutting through the centre of the city, brash and busy at all hours of the day and night, the Gran Vía is Madrid's most symbolic street. Look up as you walk along to appreciate the turrets and statues topping off the grandiose buildings. See page 30.

with the mood of the nation, the new king and his family are very popular in the country and have brought about a renewed support for the monarchy.

Felipe's older daughter Leonor is Princess and next monarch of Spain. She studied several years in Cardiff (Wales) for high school, and

Sunbathing in the Retiro Park

The Rastro market is a social event

in 2023–2024 has been receiving military instruction, both Army and Navy. She turned 18 on October 31, 2023 and swore fealty to the Spanish Constitution in the Spanish Congress on the same date.

Climate

Colder than you might expect in winter and hotter than you would think possible in summer, the Spanish capital has an extreme climate. Spring and autumn are very pleasant however – May, June, September and October are the most pleasant periods to visit. The hottest month is July, when the temperature can rise above 40°C (104°F). August is usually slightly cooler, particularly towards the end of the month. *Madrileños* leave the city in droves from mid-July onwards, often staying away for a month or more, sometimes abroad or in cooler coastal areas of Spain. Despite the low temperatures in winter, the bright light and generally clear skies make this a good time to visit, and the sunshine often warms the city up enough to sit outside during the day. January is the coldest month, when the temperature sometimes drops below 6°C (46°F). Although it rarely snows in the city, there is usually substantial snowfall in the Sierra de Guadarrama mountains to the northwest.

Population

The city of Madrid has a population of 3.46 million, while a total of 7 million people live in the Madrid region – more than double the number of inhabitants in 1950. The average age for Spanish citizens is 45, while for foreign residents it is 35. The under 15s make up 13.1 percent of the inhabitants, while 21 percent are over 65 and 6.2 percent are over 80 years old – well over half of them women.

Unlike some cities, there is no significant age difference in the various areas of Madrid. In downtown neighbourhoods such as Lavapiés, La Latina and Malasaña, communities of older people, many in flats they and their families have occupied for decades, live alongside younger residents who have moved in to enjoy the advantages of living right in the centre.

Guards at the Palacio Real

Bookshop on pasadizo de San Ginés

Until the end of the twentieth century, Madrid had a negligible number of citizens from other countries but now around 657,400 of the city inhabitants – 19 percent of the total – are from abroad. Most of the central neighbourhoods have a multicultural feel and this is particularly noticeable in Lavapiés (see page 63), where there are shops and restaurants catering to Asian and Moroccan communities. According to official census data around 38 percent of foreign residents are European, with around 18 percent Romanian; 28 percent Latin American, 12 percent African and 11 percent is of Asian origin.

Local customs

With museums and shops open until at least 8pm, the afternoon drifts well into evening, giving people an extra chunk of time in the day. While 10pm is still the norm for dinner, there is a creeping trend towards eating earlier and many restaurants take reservations from 9pm. Despite the late daily routine, with primetime television shows often ending after midnight, lots of *madrileños* start work at 9am and you need to be up early if you want to get anything done that involves bureaucracy or official organisations.

In summer, many people work what is known as a *jornada intensiva*, from 8am until 3pm, then finishing for the day. This means they can have a leisurely lunch, go to the pool or have a siesta – or maybe all three – before venturing back out when the temperature drops slightly in the evening.

While most shops and cultural centres in the city centre now open all day, smaller places still close for two or three hours in the afternoon.

Politics and economics

As the capital city, Madrid is the seat of the central government. Since June 2018, the centre-left Socialist Workers Party (PSOE) has been in power, led by prime minister Pedro Sanchez. Unemployment has been dropping steadily since the high point of 2014 (except during the two COVID years) and is now around 11.5 percent.

After years of Partido Popular control, Madrid City Council was under the leftist citizen platform Madrid Now from 2015–2019 with Manuela Carmena as mayoress. A number of ambitious – and successful – reforms were put in place: restricting private vehicles in the city centre to improve air quality and total reform of centric Plaza de España, promoting a bike share program.

In 2019 the city council returned to centre-right Partido Popular, under José Luis Martínez-Almeida Navasqüés, who was re-elected in 2023 and currently the mayor. As well as the city council, Madrid has a regional government, led by Isabel Díaz Ayuso of the Partido Popular.

Plaza Mayor is lined with pavement cafés and tapas bars

Top tips for visiting Madrid

Late habits. Expect to do everything two hours later in Madrid. A lot of museums and shops do not open until 10am and close between 8pm and 10pm, which means you can pack a lot in. Locals have lunch at 2pm and dinner at 10pm, while many bars do not liven up until after midnight.

Getting served. *Cuando puedas!* If you dread having to try and order in a frantic bar, just say this handy phrase with a wave of your hand. Pronounced *cwando pwethaz*, it means 'when you've got a minute' and is a fool-proof way to attract a busy waiter's attention without sounding rude.

Tipping. *Madrileños* leave very small tips in taxis, bars and restaurants, usually just a few coins and often nothing at all – but just leave whatever you feel comfortable with. In high-end places, however, international rules apply.

Paseo del Arte ticket. If you are planning to visit all three major museums – the Prado, Reina Sofía and Thyssen-Bornemisza – save 20 percent by buying this combined ticket, which is valid for a year, at the first one you go to (or purchase online in advance).

Free late admission. Some museums and monuments are free for the last two hours each day, including the Prado, the Reina Sofía and the Palacio Real, which is handy if you just want to see one section, or have another look at a particular work of art.

Quiet museums. While there are often queues to get into the big three art centres, there are rarely crowds in most of other museums in the city and you might even have the place to yourself. There is superb art in the Real Academia de Bellas Artes de San Fernando, Lazaro Galdiano and Cerralbo museums.

Bargain lunches. A lot of restaurants, whether basic or smart, offer a set-price deal at lunchtime called the *menu del día*. Aimed at workers rather than tourists, this usually comprises three courses and a drink and represents excellent value for money.

Shopping. Don't shop just in the streets around the Puerta del Sol. Head to Chueca, Malasaña, Conde Duque and the Barrio de las Letras for edgy independent shops and to the Salamanca area for smarter boutiques.

Beware of pickpockets. Madrid is a pretty safe city but cut down your chances of being pick-pocketed by keeping your essential belongings close to you, and leave your valuables in your hotel safe. Never leave a bag on the back of your chair in a café and you should be particularly vigilant in the metro.

Food and drink

While the Spanish capital has the most exciting food scene in Spain and one of the best in Europe, classic dishes are more popular than ever, whether strictly traditional or with a creative contemporary update.

Traditional tapas or a gastrobar? Roast pork or tuna tataki? The people of Madrid invest huge amounts of time and energy in eating and drinking in a variety of forms. If you want to understand what makes the city tick, there is no better way of going about it than doing what the locals do – which means getting used to eating later than you might normally do, both for lunch and dinner.

There are not that many spicy dishes in Spanish cooking, although chili peppers are used for some recipes, such as *gambas al ajillo* (prawns fried with chilli peppers, garlic and parsley).

While a lot of Spanish restaurants in other countries focus on tapas, in Madrid it is actually just as usual to go for a sit-down meal – although that might well involve sharing dishes, too.

After decades of sticking stubbornly with the tried and tested, foreign influences are flooding into the city. A new generation of chefs and foodies is bringing fresh ideas to the table – literally – from what they have learned on their travels around the globe. This means juice bars, a trend towards healthier food and a much-improved vegetarian scene. Spanish cuisine is not losing its essence, however, as chefs are using the experiences gained abroad to put a new spin on what is known as *la cocina de la abuela*, or grandmother's cooking, reinventing dishes to appeal to modern palates.

Madrilenian specialities

Purists will be pleased to learn that traditional restaurants are still flourishing, priding themselves on the quality of their roast meats, particularly lamb and suckling pig, which are cooked in huge wood-burning ovens.

Madrid's most characteristic dish is not paella but *cocido madrileño*, a robust stew that has evolved from the *olla podrida* and the Jewish *adafina* of medieval times. Made with chickpeas, pork, beef, chorizo sausage, cabbage, leeks, noodles and quite a few more things too, it is served in stages: first the broth with vermicelli in it, then the various vegetables and finally the meats and sausages.

Another speciality is *callos a la madrileña*, which is tripe cooked in a tomato sauce with *pimentón*, the Spanish version of paprika. Both are more suited to winter, as is *sopa castellana*, a warming soup made with the simplest

Spanish paella

of ingredients: meat stock, garlic, bread, *pimentón* paprika and eggs.

Madrid may be hundreds of kilometres from the sea but fish and seafood are superb, having been transported in refrigerated trucks or planes from the Atlantic and the Mediterranean. *Madrileños* love bream and hake, while one of the most typical things to eat in the city is the *bocadillo de calamares*, a chunky roll stuffed with squid rings in batter.

Tapas

To do things properly, tapas should ideally be consumed standing up and shared between two or more people. Order a couple of tapas at each place, with a beer or a glass of wine, then move on to somewhere else, going to at least three or four in an evening.

A tapa is usually a very small portion. If you are sharing between several people, order a *media ración* or a *ración*. Just look around at what other people are having and don't be afraid to ask them what it is – that is all part of the fun. It is not obligatory to move from place to place, however. If you are comfortable where you are, just stay put.

Where to eat

With a few days in Madrid, you could have a meal at a classic restaurant, eat at a few informal places with modern cuisine and have a couple of evenings on a tapas crawl down Cava Baja or around Plaza Santa Ana.

Provided you are not too fussy, do as the *madrileños* do and have a set-price lunch wherever you happen to be.

Traditional restaurants

If you like good quality, no-nonsense food, be sure to have a meal at one of the restaurants near the Plaza Mayor. While **Botín** (see page 99) is the most famous – and the oldest – **Casa Lucío** (see page 37) is a good option, as is **Los Galayos** (see page 99). While these all specialise in roast suckling pig and lamb, there are plenty of other options on the menu if that is not your thing.

Tapas bars

There is quite a contrast between the tapas bars that have been around for decades and the more modern gastrobars, which started emerging in the late 1990s and are now an established part of the gastronomic scene. Try traditional tapas at **El Lacón** (see page 101), **La Bodega de la Ardosa** (see page 102). For a more contemporary vibe, grab a stool at **Angelita** (see page 102) or **La Dichosa** (see page 103).

Modern Spanish restaurants

Madrid is particularly strong on less formal places where the focus is on the fresh flavours and less fuss. With a younger vibe and pared-back décor, these restaurants are usually run by talented young chefs with

Traditional roast lamb

Typical tapas dishes

creative ideas and are often excellent value. **La Vinoteca de Moratín** (see page 53) and **Triciclo** (see page 102) are good options.

Michelin stars

There are 26 Michelin-starred restaurants in the Madrid region, but David Muñoz is the only chef to have won three stars. Eating at his restaurant **DiverXo** (see page 105), where the astonishing cuisine mixes Spanish and Asian influences, is as much a theatrical as a gastronomic experience. Muñoz also runs the **StreetXo** bar at **Gourmet Experience** (see page 105), where anyone can try his zingy dishes if they don't mind queuing.

The six restaurants with two Michelin stars include **Ramon Freixa Madrid** (see page 105) and Paco Roncero's **La Terraza del Casino** (see page 99). Eight places have one star, including *Cebo* at *Hotel Urban*, which received theirs in 2024 (see page 101).

Drinks

Wine

Many bars sell a good range of quality wine by the glass – it's a perfect opportunity to try reds from regions such as Ribera del Duero, El Bierzo or Priorat and whites from Rueda, Rías Baixas or Alella. You should also try wines made in the Madrid region, such as those from the organic winery Bodega Saavedra in Cenicientos in

> ## Food and drink prices
>
> The price guide is based on a two-course meal with one glass of wine:
> €€€€ = more than 60 euros
> €€€ = 40–60 euros
> €€ = 25–40 euros
> € = less than 25 euros

the southwest. In warm weather a refreshing choice is *tinto de verano*, which is simply red wine topped up with lemonade over lots of ice in a long glass, much more popular than *sangría* and usually available at pavement cafés.

Vermouth

Something you really should get your head around in Madrid is the *hora del aperitivo*. This is the hour, sometime after noon/before lunch, to devote to having a civilized drink, preferably the local red vermouth, although beer and wine are acceptable too, accompanied by a few tasty bites. Although it never really went away, vermouth is very much in fashion. Vermut Zarro is made in Madrid and is often available on draught in bars and restaurants.

Beer

Lager-style beer is tremendously popular, particularly Mahou, which is brewed in Madrid. Locals usually ask for a *caña*, which is a small glass of draught beer. If you want something bigger, ask for a *doble*. Craft beers are

San Miguel market was one of the first gourmet markets

Gourmet markets

In the last decade, a different sort of market has been emerging all over Madrid. Some are revamps of existing food markets, while others are totally new. Some mix fruit and vegetable stalls with tapas bars, others are more like gastronomic food courts. All are dynamic spaces where visitors can taste all sorts of local produce as well as wines from all over the country. You just graze around the stalls picking up what you fancy then find yourself a table.

The trend was kick-started by the Mercado de San Miguel (see page 33), which opened in 2009 by the Plaza Mayor. While the Mercado de Antón Martín (calle Santa Isabel 5, www.mercadoantonmartin.com) is still very much a local market, now sushi and smoothies are on offer too. The Mercado de San Ildefonso (calle Fuencarral 57; mercadodesanildefonso. com), between fashionable Chueca and Malasaña, is packed out in the evenings and at weekends. Nearby, the Mercado de San Antón (see page 67) combines tapas places and deli stalls with a great restaurant and a groovy bar up on the roof terrace. Originally a cinema, Platea (see page 78) is where well-groomed *madrileños* take a break from the designer boutiques on nearby Serrano street.

increasingly common, with several brewed in or around the city. Look out for Cervezas La Cibeles, Madriz Hop Republic, Patanel or Cerveza Enigma.

Mixed drinks

Copas, as mixed drinks are known, and gin and tonics are incredibly popular, often served in huge balloon glasses. State the brand of gin, whisky, vodka or whatever that you want, otherwise you might be served one of dubious quality.

Coffee

Coffee is invariably made in an espresso machine, usually using high-roast beans. Asking for *un café* or *un solo* will get you a straight espresso. *Café con leche* is a shot of espresso with about twice the quantity of hot milk. *Un cortado* is espresso with just a dash of hot milk. A *carajillo* is black coffee with a slug of brandy (or whatever you prefer).

Soft drinks

A wide range is available, including beer (*cerveza sin alcohol*). Surprisingly, orange juice is not always fresh, so specify *natural* when ordering. In summer, try a *granizado de limón* – lemon juice blended with crushed ice and sugar – or *horchata*, a concoction of *chufas*, the tubers grown in the Valencia region known as tiger nuts, mixed with crushed ice and sugar.

Typical bars serve locally brewed and craft beers

Shopping

While Spanish brands seem to be taking over high streets all over Europe and beyond, there is a lot more to shopping in Madrid than the familiar names, with independent boutiques and traditional shops all over town.

What to buy

Department stores sit alongside tiny shops that just sell umbrellas, espadrilles or gloves in the centre of Madrid, where shopping is an activity to be enjoyed rather than endured. Spain has a long tradition of making good-quality shoes and bags and there is a wide range of both classic and contemporary designs on offer. Expect to pay high prices for handmade items, however.

Gourmet foods make good gifts and are widely available at specialist shops, department stores and gastronomic markets (see page 19). Look out for *pimentón* paprika in pretty tins, olive oil, sherry vinegar, *turrón* nougat and chocolates. *Ibérico* ham, *chorizo* and other charcuterie, as well as cheeses, can usually be vacuum packed.

While larger stores and boutiques stay open all day – including Sundays – usually from 9.30am until 8.30pm, small shops close from 2pm to 5pm. All over the city, you will have no difficulty finding convenience stores that sell mineral water as well as other drinks and snacks.

Where to buy

Around the Puerta del Sol and Gran Vía

The pedestrianised area between the Puerta del Sol and the Gran Vía, formed by calle Preciados and adjoining streets, is packed with mainstream clothes and shoe shops, such as Zara, Mango and Camper, and this is where the original branch of El Corte Inglés department store is situated. FNAC (calle Preciados 28) is a very useful store for books (including in English), music and any bits and pieces you might need for your phone or camera. The Casa del Libro (Gran Vía 29) is a huge bookshop with an English section and a wide variety of guidebooks and books on Madrid. Casa Diego (Puerta del Sol 12) has been in business since 1858 and specialises in handmade fans. Nearby at calle Cruz 23, Capas Seseña has been making capes for more than a century.

Around the Plaza Mayor and Madrid de los Austrias

The Austrias neighbourhood behind the Plaza Mayor around calle Toledo has the densest concentration of

A colourful display of fans

Leather sandals at the Rastro market

traditional old shops with wooden frontages and painted glass signs, but these are sadly disappearing fast. For a huge range of traditional espadrilles and a mind-boggling array of other rope-related items, don't miss Casa Hernanz (calle Toledo 18). For classic hats and shawls, browse around the porticoed galleries of the Plaza Mayor.

Calle Serrano and Salamanca area

The smartest shops are in the grid of streets in the Salamanca district, where all the well-known chain stores are also present. Calle Serrano and calle Goya both have an upmarket high street feel, while Claudio Coello, Lagasca and Jorge Juan streets are quieter but also packed with boutiques. On calle Serrano, look out for Manolo

Blahnik, who was born in La Palma in the Canary Islands and has an elegant shop at No. 58. Ágatha Ruíz de La Prada, one of Spain's best-known designers, has her shop at No. 27, with brightly coloured clothes for adults and children. Calle José Ortega y Gasset is lined with top international names, such as Christian Dior (No. 6), and Chanel (No.16). Lavinia (No. 16) is a fabulous wine shop with a gastrobar upstairs. The Mercado de la Paz (calle Ayala 28B) is a great food market with delicatessen stalls.

Around calle Fuencarral

The pedestrianised street is lined with shops, including Desigual, Muji and Mac. Calle Augusto Figueroa, which is known for its outlet shoe shops, runs through Chueca to the Salesas area, where Barquillo, Almirante and Conde de Xiquena are the streets to explore for upmarket independent boutiques.

In Malasaña, the liveliest streets for shopping are Corredera Alta de San Pablo, Espíritu Santo, Manuela Malasaña and cross streets. At calle Divino Pastor No. 29, family-run Antigua Casa Crespo was founded in 1865 and specialises in espadrilles of every description.

In the lower part of the neighbourhood, nearer the Gran Vía, *madrileño* hipsters hunt for vintage treasures in the edgier Triball area, trawling the boutiques and galleries on Valverde and Pez streets.

The bustling shopping street, calle Fuencarral

Entertainment

Madrid nightlife is hectic, fast-moving and carries on all night. Gregarious at heart, *madrileños* are night creatures, hopping in and out of tabernas, restaurants and bars. But they are also a sophisticated bunch, and cultural distractions are plentiful.

It often seems that the entire population is on the streets after dark in Madrid. Every night there is a huge range of theatre, music and dance events to choose from, with something to suit all tastes and budgets. Throughout the summer, there are performances at outdoor venues all over the city, often at very reasonable prices.

While you usually need to book ahead for the opera or major concerts, for the majority of events you can buy tickets on the day or just turn up. An easy way to find out what is on is to look at the What's On section of the Madrid tourism website (www.esmadrid. es/en) or Leisure time guide (https:// guiadelocio.es/madrid). Information on individual venues is given in the Nightlife section (see page 106).

Theatre

Madrid's theatre tradition can be traced back to the Golden Age in the seventeenth century (see page 58). Classic and contemporary Spanish plays are still performed in the same area as the original courtyard venues, at the Teatro Nacional (see page 58) and the Teatro de la Comedia (calle

Príncipe 14; https://teatroclasico.mcu. es/la-comp/teatro-de-la-comedia), as well as the Centro Dramático Nacional (National Dramatic Centre) with theatres María Guerrero (calle Tamayo y Beus 4) and Valle-Inclán (Plaza Lavapies), program for both at https://dramatico.mcu.es/en/.

Once the Broadway of Madrid, the Gran Vía has lost a lot of its theatres, but several on the stretch from Plaza de Callao to Plaza de España are still going strong by staging major musicals, such as *The Lion King* or *The Phantom of the Opera*.

Classical music and opera

While it is a very special experience to see an opera or a concert at the magnificent Teatro Real (see page 40), it is also interesting to see the more typically *madrileño* form of light opera, known as *zarzuela*, whether at the Teatro de la Zarzuela (see page 106) or in one of the city's parks or gardens in summer. The main venue for classical music is the splendid Auditorio Nacional de Música (see page 106), with regular concerts by Spanish and international orchestras and performers.

A well-attended corrida in the prestigious Las Ventas bullring

Jazz, rock and pop

There is a variety of live music every night in the city, whether large-scale concerts by major artists or more intimate events in small theatres, cultural centres and clubs. Throughout the summer months individual concerts and festivals are held outdoors too, often in magical settings. A jazz festival is staged in November at the Centro Cultural Conde Duque (see page 67), where there are regular concerts of all sorts of music.

Dance

Madrid has a dynamic dance scene, ranging from classical to contemporary. The Ballet Nacional de España, which focuses on Spanish styles, and the more experimental Compañía Nacional de Danza perform at several theatres, including the Teatro Real. The Víctor Ullate Ballet – Comunidad de Madrid company is based at the Teatros del Canal. Other key venues include the Teatro Albéniz, the Teatro Fernán Gómez (see page 75) and the Matadero cultural centre.

Flamenco

While Andalucía is the home of flamenco, its best exponents perform regularly in Madrid, giving visitors a chance to experience both the traditional and contemporary versions of this extraordinary art. It can be tricky as a visitor to find truly authentic flamenco, as the best tend to be both unplanned and private, but the city has several venues run by flamenco artists where you can see top-quality musicians and dancers (see page 107).

Bullfighting

Bullfighting continues to be an important part of Spanish life. Although many Spaniards do not support it, the *aficionados* are fiercely passionate about the whole culture surrounding it. Madrid's main bullring, Las Ventas, is one of the largest and most prestigious in the world. The season runs from March to October, but the most exciting periods, with top matadors appearing every evening, are the San Isidro festival in May and the Otoño (Autumn) festival at the end of September.

Nightlife

Nightlife is just life in Madrid, as this is a city where staying out late is the norm rather than the exception. If you just go out for dinner and a drink or two afterwards you will be lucky to get to bed before 2am. Any time before that is regarded as an early night. Going out is not restricted to millennials either – you see people of all ages enjoying a drink with friends in both the most traditional and the most fashionable bars.

Lively areas at night include Plaza de Santa Ana, Malasaña and La Latina (around Cava Baja and Plaza de la Paja). A lot of bars have to close at 2am – regulations are very strict – but there is no shortage of places that stay open later.

Choose from a variety of bars in the old town for after-dinner drinks

Chronology

While its origins as a Muslim settlement by the Manzanares River were humble, Madrid started growing fast after becoming the capital of Spain in the mid-sixteenth century, acquiring the dynamic character that survives to this day.

Early history

852 The Emir of Córdoba, Mohammed I, builds the Alcázar fortress where the Almudena cathedral is now.

1085 Alfonso VI negotiates a surrender of Toledo city-state with king Al-Qadir, bringing Madrid under Christian control and moving the Christian – Muslim border to the Tagus River.

1202 Alfonso VIII grants Madrid its own *fuero* (statutes), formalising town laws and rights.

1369 The foundation of the Trastámara dynasty consolidates Madrid's position with the embellishment of the Alcázar.

1474 Beginning of consolidated rule of the Catholic Monarchs, Isabel I of Castile and Fernando of Aragón over most of the peninsula, with an itinerant capital city.

1492 "Reconquest" against Muslim rule ends with Granada's surrender. Jews expelled; Christopher Columbus discovers the New World in the name of Spain.

Habsburg Madrid and the Golden Age

1516 The Habsburg period begins when Carlos I, Holy Roman Emperor, is crowned king of Spain.

1561 Felipe II establishes capital in Madrid, replacing Toledo.

1563 Building of El Escorial begins.

1547 Birth of the writer Miguel de Cervantes.

1601–06 Madrid renamed capital after brief stint in Valladolid.

1617–19 Construction of the Plaza Mayor.

1621–65 Reign of Felipe IV.

1623 Diego de Velázquez is appointed court painter.

1625 Work begins on the fourth and final city wall, demolished in 1860.

1632 The Buen Retiro Palace is built.

Bourbon Madrid

1701–14 War of Spanish Succession; start of the Bourbon rule.

1738 Construction of the royal palace begins after 1734 fire destroys the Alcázar.

1746 Birth of the painter Francisco Goya.

1752 Foundation of the Real Academia de Bellas Artes de San Fernando; reign of Fernando VI.

1759–88 Reign of Carlos III, the 'mayor-king'; major urban development.

Goya's The San Isidro Meadow (1788) – a panoramic view of Madrid

1808 Carlos IV abdicates; Madrid revolts against the French army.
1808–14 Peninsula War; Joseph Bonaparte becomes king.
1814–33 Reign of Fernando VII.
1819 The Prado Museum opens.
1836 State confiscation; demolition of monasteries and convents in city centre.
1851 First train service from Madrid to Aranjuez.
1874 Restoration of the Bourbon monarchy.

Twentieth century

1910 Building work starts on the Gran Vía.
1919 The metro underground system opens.
1931 Abdication of Alfonso XIII; start of the Second Republic.
1936–39 Spanish Civil War.
1939–75 Dictatorship of General Francisco Franco.
1975 Juan Carlos I is crowned King of Spain.
1978 December 6: Spanish Constitution is passed by referendum.
1979 Enrique Tierno Galván is elected mayor of Madrid and La Movida creative movement emerges.
1981 Colonel Tejero storms the Cortes parliament building in a failed military coup.
1982 Socialist Workers Party (PSOE) wins elections, returning left-center to power for the first time after Franco's dictatorship.
1986 Spain joins the European Union.

Twenty-first century

2004 Terrorist attack on commuter trains results in 201 deaths.
2011 The Indignados movement occupies the Puerta del Sol, protesting against unemployment, corruption and the establishment.
2013 Guadarrama Mountains National Park is declared, with most of it located in Madrid, and a portion in Segovia.
2014 King Juan Carlos I abdicates and his son becomes king as Felipe VI.
2015 Manuela Carmena of the Ahora Madrid (Madrid Now) citizen platform becomes mayoress.
2017 The Spanish government, based in Madrid, clamps down on Catalonia's bid for independence.
2018 Under Manuela Carmena, introduction of first restrictions on private vehicle circulation in central Madrid, to comply with EU clean air mandate.
2020 COVID outbreak begins, leading to strict confinement mid-March to mid-May.
2021 January 7–9 Filomena blizzard dumps 50cm of snow on Madrid, paralyzing the city for a week. World Heritage site declared: Landscape of Light, Retiro and Paseo del Prado.
2023 October 31. Princess Leonor, future queen of Spain, swore allegiance to uphold the Spanish Constitution on her 18th birthday.
2024 Real Madrid wins UEFA Champions League.

TRIP PLANS

WALK 1
Puerta del Sol and the Gran Vía

Tracing the triangle from the Puerta del Sol along Calle de Alcalá and back along the Gran Vía, this short walk through the core of the city helps you get your bearings and includes some of Madrid's best-known landmarks.

> **DISTANCE:** 2.5km (1.5 miles)
> **TIME:** 2 hours
> **START/END:** Puerta del Sol
> **POINTS TO NOTE:** This easy walk is good to do on arrival and combines well with walks 2, 7 and 9. Beware of pickpockets in the Puerta del Sol and along the Gran Vía, which are always crowded.

Walking towards Puerta del Sol along calle de Alcalá, you'll see the grand architectural styles of the late nineteenth and early twentieth centuries. Many were originally banks, illustrating how Madrid developed commercially in that period. Nowadays, these streets are lined with shops and cafés, and a few cultural institutions too.

Puerta del Sol

The **Puerta del Sol** ❶ is the heart of Madrid and has one of the city's busiest metro stations. The name means Gate of the Sun and comes from the eastern gate in the fifteenth-century city wall.

While the city's intellectuals used to meet at cafés here, now most people just rush through, clutching bags from shops in the surrounding streets. People do congregate here, however, for protests and demonstrations, and on New Year's Eve, for the ritual of eating a grape with each chime as the clock strikes midnight.

Sol has had a variety of configurations since its first big revamp in the 1800s – most recently in October 2023. However, a few things are still pending, including the promised removal of the "Glass Whale" (entrance to the metro and commuter train), to be replaced by something smaller and more functional.

Casa de Correos

The red-brick clock tower crowns the **Casa de Correos**, built in 1768 as the central post office, now the headquarters of the regional government. The popular uprising against Napoleon's army took place in front of the building on May 2, 1808. The following day, hundreds of people were shot here in cold blood, a scene immortalised by Spanish painter, Francisco de Goya.

The Puerta del Sol, Madrid's busiest square

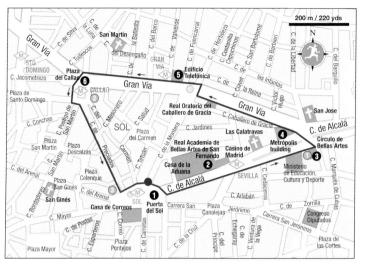

Kilómetro Cero

Look down at the pavement in front of the building, where a semicircular plaque marks "Kilometre Zero", the official marker for Spain's six radial highways (A1 to A6). It also indicates directions to most major cities in Spain.

El Oso y Madroño

Sol's most popular feature is the bronze statue of a bear leaning on an arbutus (or wild strawberry) tree. Madrid's most famous – and most photographed – symbol features on the city's coat of arms.

The equestrian statue on the west side is of King Carlos III and is a relatively recent addition (1997).

Calle de Alcalá

Stretching east from the Puerta del Sol, calle de Alcalá originated as the ceremonial royal route to the historic town of Alcalá de Henares, 35km (22 miles) away. At the turn of the twentieth century, the street was Madrid's financial hub.

Real Academia de Bellas Artes de San Fernando

On the left at No. 13 is the **Real Academia de Bellas Artes de San Fernando ②** (Royal Academy of Fine Arts of San Fernando; www.rabasf.com; charge). This museum holds thirteen paintings by Goya, as well as works by El Greco, Zurbarán, Rubens and Picasso.

The opulent building next door is the **Casino de Madrid**, built in 1910. While this is a private club, anyone can book a table at *La Terraza* restaurant on the top floor (see page 99).

Up ahead on the right, on the corner of calle Sevilla, raise your gaze to see two chariots, each drawn by four horses, galloping into the sky. On the left is the seventeenth-century Baroque church of **Las Calatravas** (www.iglesiacalatravas. com; free), with an ornate altarpiece by José Benito de Churriguera.

Círculo de Bellas Artes

On the right at No. 42 stands the **Círculo de Bellas Artes ❸** (Fine Arts Circle; www.circulobellasartes.com; charge), a popular cultural centre that was designed by Antonio Palacios in 1920. Zoom up to the Azotea roof terrace for panoramic views. **La Pecera** café, see ❶, on the ground floor is a good place for a coffee.

Further down the street, you can see Plaza de Cibeles (see page 44) with the Puerta de Alcalá on the hill beyond (see page 54).

The **Metrópolis ❹** building stands at the apex of the chevron-shaped junction of calle Alcalá and Gran Vía. Designed by Jules and Raymond Février between 1907–10, it has a striking facade with a bronze figure of the Winged Victory on top of the slate dome.

Cross to the north side of the junction, with a quick stop on the island to inspect the model of the Gran Vía,

depicting all of the iconic buildings from here to Plaza de España. On the north side of the street, admire the **Iglesia de San José** (www.esmadrid.com; free), which dates back to the 1730s and was designed by Pedro de Ribera.

Gran Vía

The capital's most famous street was developed in the early twentieth century. People flocked there to admire the grand buildings, or go to the theatres and fashionable cafés. Nowadays, you will see more chain boutiques and fast-food joints, but it still teems with life at all hours.

The curved, colonnaded facade of the Grassy jeweller's heralds the beginning of the avenue. The architects were keen to emulate the elegant Paris boulevards created by Haussmann. On the right at No. 12 is the legendary **Museo Chicote** cocktail bar (see page 107), which dates back to the 1930s.

Oratorio del Caballero de Gracia

On the left at No. 17 is the curving rear facade of the restored **Real Oratorio del Caballero de Gracia** (https://caballerodegracia.org; free). Designed by Juan de Villanueva at the end of the eighteenth century, it is one of the best examples of neoclassical architecture in the city.

The junction with Montera, Hortaleza and Fuencarral streets marks the start of the second section of the Gran Vía, which was built in

The Burial of the Sardine (1819), by Goya

the 1920s. The architecture on this stretch combines Art Deco features with the American influences.

The entrance to the Gran Via metro station is a reproduction of the original designed by Antonio Palacios. The station was modernised and during that process some historical research was conducted, partially visible around the station escalators up to street level.

The Telefónica building
The massive structure on the right is the **Edificio Telefónica** ❺ headquarters of Spain's main telecommunications' company. Madrid's first skyscraper, it is 88 metres (289 ft) tall and was designed by the American architect Louis S. Weeks. It also houses the **Fundación Telefónica** (https://espacio.fundaciontelefonica.com; free), which has an outstanding art collection. War correspondents (including Ernest Hemingway) used this building during the Civil War.

Shops have replaced most of the theatres that characterised the avenue until the early twenty-first century. Join the crowds walking along to the **Plaza del Callao** ❻. The curved Art Deco facade up ahead is the Carrión building by Martínez Fecuchi y Vicente Eced, which houses the *Capitol* hotel and cinema. For a drink with a view, go up to **Gourmet Experience**, see ❷, on the top floor of **El Corte Inglés** (Calle de Raimundo Fernández Villaverde).

Food and drink

❶ La Pecera
Círculo de Bellas Artes, Calle Alcalá 42; www.lapeceradelcirculo.com; €
This grand café, decorated with chandeliers, paintings and a marble statue, is an impressive place for breakfast.

❷ Gourmet Experience
El Corte Inglés, Plaza de Callao 2; www.esmadrid.com; €
This food court on the ninth floor has a variety of outlets to suit all tastes, as well as speciality foods that make good gifts.

❸ Casa Labra
Calle Tetuán 12; www.casalabra.es; €
Established in 1860, this traditional tavern is where Pablo Iglesias founded the Spanish Socialist Workers' Party (PSOE) in 1879. The cod strips in batter are very popular here.

Calle Preciados
Turn left down calle Preciados, which leads back down to the Puerta del Sol. After passing another large El Corte Inglés, turn right into calle Tetuán to reach **Casa Labra** tapas bar, see ❸, which is an excellent place to end your walk, with excellent tapas and draught beer.

Gran Vía and calle Alcalá crossroads at dusk

WALK 2
Plaza Mayor and Madrid de los Austrias

Madrid de Los Austrias – or Habsburg Madrid – is the oldest part of the city. While not many buildings survive from the medieval period, it is easy to trace the capital's history in the narrow streets, which are still full of character.

DISTANCE: 2.5km (1.5 miles)
TIME: 3 hours
START: Plaza Mayor
END: Plaza de Santa Cruz
POINTS TO NOTE: You could do this walk in the morning, visiting the museums and churches, then again in the evening, going to tapas bars along the way. The streets are very atmospheric at dusk.

The Habsburgs reigned in Madrid from 1561, when the city became the capital of Spain, to 1700. This was the Golden Age, when Madrid was the headquarters of the Spanish Empire following the discovery of the Americas.

Plaza Mayor

You can soak up four hundred years of history in the **Plaza Mayor** ❶. Framed by elegant red buildings with slate roofs and spindly spires – traditional Habsburg architectural features – the

elegant square may no longer be the hub of city life that it once was, but it is still used for events, including a Christmas market. Cafés sprawl across the cobbles, bars and shops line the arcades.

Designed by Juan Gómez de Mora in 1617, over the centuries it has been used for bullfights, as a theatre for plays, for jousting, and the sinister trials known as *autos-da-fé*, held by the Inquisition. The height of the buildings was revolutionary at the time and housed around 3,000 citizens, inspiring a lot of jokes about people living on top of each other.

Following a fire at the end of the eighteenth century, the square was redesigned by Juan de Villanueva, the architect of the Prado Museum, who added the entrance arches and made the buildings the same height. The equestrian statue in the middle of the square is of Felipe III.

The frescoes on the north side of the square were created relatively recently, in 1992, by Carlos Franco, and decorate the building known as

Stalls at the San Miguel market

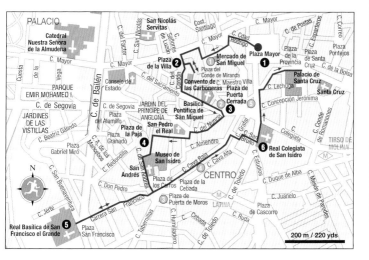

the Casa de la Panaderia, originally the headquarters of the bakers' guild. Nowadays, the ground floor houses the city's main tourist information centre.

Mercado de San Miguel

Leave the Plaza Mayor through the arch in the northwestern corner, walking along calle Ciudad Rodrigo, and you'll see people streaming in and out of the **Mercado de San Miguel**, see ①. The dainty glass and ironwork structure, which dates back to 1916, housed a neighbourhood market for nearly a century – until it was turned into a gastronomic hub in 2009. An instant success, it was the catalyst for the trend for gourmet markets in Madrid and indeed throughout Spain.

Plaza de la Villa

Walk along calle Mayor to the elegant **Plaza de la Villa** ②, which was the most important square in medieval Madrid. The seventeenth-century **Casa de la Villa** (on the right looking from the calle Mayor) is one of the key buildings of Habsburg Madrid, designed by Juan Gómez de Mora. Until 2007 it housed the City Hall, which then moved to the Palacio de Cibeles (see page 45). Opposite is the **Torre y Casa de los Lujanes**, dating back to the time of the Catholic Monarchs in the late fifteenth-century. The main door in Gothic style was added in the 1920s, but the arch on the right is the work of Mudéjar artisans.

If you walk down the narrow calle del Codo – meaning "elbow" in Spanish

Plaza de la Villa

and curving around the building – you come to the Plaza del Conde de Miranda, with the seventeenth-century **Convento de las Carboneras** on the right (free), which gets its name from an image of the Virgin that was found in a coal yard. The nuns make their own cakes, which you can buy by means of a rotating drum called a *torno* – this is a closed order so the nuns cannot be seen.

Returning to the Plaza de la Villa, at the bottom of the square is the Plateresque **Casa de Cisneros**, built in the 1500s for the nephew of Cardinal Cisneros. It was remodelled in the early twentieth century as an addition to the Casa de la Villa. At Christmas, this building might be used to show an elaborate *Belén* (Nativity Scene)

Basílica Pontífica de San Miguel

Cut down the side of the building to **calle Sacramento**, one of the best-preserved streets in Madrid. Turning left, the street becomes calle San Justo, with the **Basílica Pontífica de San Miguel** (www.bsmiguel.es; free) on the left. Built in the mid-eighteenth century, the Baroque church was designed by Giacomo Bonavia and features circular vaults over the single nave. Also from that period is the **Palacio Arzobispal** (Archbishop's Palace) next door.

Plaza de Puerta Cerrada

Continue along calle San Justo to reach **Plaza de Puerta Cerrada ❸**,

the site of another medieval city gate but now better known for its striking murals, added in the 1980s by Alberto Corazón. A few traditional shops survive in and around the square, a vestige of those who came from every region to sell and buy tools and supplies such as sieves and ropes. On the left at No. 11 is the brightly-painted wooden facade of **Casa Paco**, see ❷, one of the city's most traditional taverns and a good spot for a cold beer and a tapa.

Cross calle Segovia at the traffic lights, bear a little to the right and turn left into the narrow calle del Nuncio, which is lined with palatial residences, now mostly official buildings. At the end you come upon the **Iglesia de San Pedro el Viejo** (www.esmadrid. com; free), founded in the mid-fourteenth century but largely rebuilt in the seventeenth century. The brick tower with loophole windows is one of the few examples of Mudéjar architecture in Madrid. The church's statue, Jesús el Pobre, is one of the best-loved statues and processions during Madrid's Easter Week celebration.

Plaza de la Paja

Walk down the pedestrianised calle Príncipe de Anglona to the **Plaza de la Paja ❹**. At the end of the street and the bottom of the square, is the **Jardín del Príncipe de Anglona** (free) a tiny yet delightful garden created in the eighteenth century and laid out in its current form in 1920.

The delightful Jardín del Príncipe de Anglona

The sloping Plaza de la Paja looks calm now, with its café terraces under the trees, but in early Christian times this was the heart of Madrid and in the Middle Ages the wealthiest families lived in palaces around the square.

Workers from the fields down by the river had to donate a tenth of their crop to the **Iglesia de San Andrés** (www.esmadrid.com; free), which dominates the top of the space (entrance on Plaza de San Andrés). The church was founded in the thirteenth century, rebuilt in the seventeenth, then severely damaged by fire in the Civil War.

The part of the structure giving onto the square is the late-Gothic **Capilla del Obispo** (www.esmadrid.com/en/tourist-information/capilla-del-obispo-en-la-iglesia-de-san-andres; free) with its extraordinarily ornate Plateresque decoration. This chapel has a convent, home to a small order of nuns.

The square with four names

Walking out of the square around the side of the church brings you to a space that has four different names: this part is **Plaza de los Carros**, after the wagons and stagecoaches that used to arrive here from Toledo and all around Spain. To the south it is the **Puerta de Moros**, after a city gate that stood here, while to the left is the **Plaza del Humilladero**. By the entrance to the church, it is the **Plaza de San Andrés**. There are lots of pavement cafés and restaurants in the square, including **AltoBardero**,

San Isidro Labrador

Isidro was a hardworking youth, born in the late eleventh century, who toiled in the fields on the far side of the Manzanares River. When he fell asleep on the job, angels apparently descended to plough the field for him. When Ivan Vargas, his boss, turned up on a sweltering day, Isidro somehow made a spring of cool water gush forth from the ground. Perhaps most miraculous of all, when Isidro's wife dropped their baby down a well, Isidro made the water rise up, with the baby bobbing on the surface. He was beatified in 1618 and canonised four years later. His feast day is May 15: a public holiday in Madrid with festivities going on throughout the month.

see ❸, where you can have a drink with a tapa or a sit-down meal.

Museo de San Isidro

Just beyond the church on Plaza de San Andrés the **Museo de San Isidro** (www.madrid.es; free) charts Madrid's origins from prehistoric times until the establishment of the court in the 1500s and gives a useful overview of how the city developed over the centuries. Don't miss the section on the city walls, with an interesting model of the medieval city. The **Museo de la Historia de Madrid** in walk 9 (see page 65) deals with later periods in Madrid's history.

The curving calle Cava Baja

It is claimed that Madrid's patron saint, San Isidro Labrador (St Isidore the Labourer), lived in a house on this site and the final section of the displays deals with his life and the many miracles he performed (see box). Fragments remain from the sixteenth and seventeenth centuries, including the Renaissance courtyard and the chapel.

Real Basílica de San Francisco el Grande

From the square, you could make a short detour down Carrera de San Francisco to see the **Real Basílica de San Francisco el Grande 5** (www. esmadrid.com; charge), one of the most important churches in the city.

Legend has it that St. Francis of Assisi founded a chapel here in 1217. This much grander structure was built in the mid-eighteenth century, although construction was beset by problems owing to the massive dome, which has a span of 33 metres (108 ft) and is 56 metres (184 ft) high, one of the widest church domes in the world. The first chapel on the left as you enter features an early work by Goya, showing St. Bernardino of Siena. Goya included himself in the painting, on the right wearing a yellow jacket. There are also paintings by Zurbarán and Alonso Cano.

Cava Baja

Return to San Andrés square. To your right, the large building with coloured domes is La Cebada market, a typical market with a wide variety of products, but not a gastronomic experience like San Miguel. Exit the square at the top end of curving **calle Cava Baja**, which follows the course of the ditch around the twelfth-century city wall. Inns sprang up in medieval times to accommodate the merchants and travellers from the stagecoaches and to this day the street is lined with bars and restaurants. The most famous is **Casa Lucio** at No. 35, see **4**, which has been open for more than forty years. Workshops occupied for centuries by saddlers, coopers and basket makers have now mostly disappeared, replaced by gastrobars, but the street still has a medieval atmosphere.

Real Colegiata de San Isidro

Turn right on calle San Bruno, which brings you to calle Toledo and the **Real Colegiata de San Isidro 6** (www.es madrid.com; free). This was Madrid's cathedral until the Almudena (see page 42) opened in 1994 and for many is still the most important church.

The Baroque structure was built in 1622 and was originally a Jesuit church. While the original design was by Pedro Sánchez, Francisco Bautista devised the large slate dome and Ventura Rodríguez undertook a neoclassical restoration in the eighteenth century, when it was renamed after San Isidro and the saint's remains were brought from the San Andrés church.

View of the Real Colegiata de San Isidro from Plaza Mayor

Food and drink

❶ Mercado de San Miguel
Plaza de San Miguel;
www.mercadodesanmiguel.es; €€
This traditional market is now a gourmet
food court that is packed at all hours
with everyone clutching glasses of wine,
vermouth or beer and plates of prawns,
oysters, cheese, ham and lots more.

❷ Casa Paco
Plaza Puerta Cerrada 11;
www.casapaco1933.es; €€
Open since the 1930s, Casa Paco is
one of the most traditional places
for Madrilenian specialities or a
cold beer and a tapa at the bar.

❸ AltoBardero
Puerta de Moros 4; €€
A new tapas bar in the same location
as the previous (and famous) *Juana*

la Loca, with some of the same
staff and an updated menu that
still includes their famous tortilla
omelette, and a new wine list.

❹ Casa Lucio
Cava Baja 35; www.casalucio.es; €€€
This classic Castilian restaurant is a
real Madrid institution and attracts a
glamorous clientele who come here
for the roast meats from the wood-
fired oven and the legendary *huevos
rotos* – fried eggs on a pile of chips.

❺ El Madroño
Calle Latoneros 10 and
Plaza Puerta Cerrada 7;
https://grupoelmadrono.com; €€
These two tile-fronted restaurants
have a good selection of tapas and
classic Spanish dishes. Both have
outdoor seating areas. There is another
El Madroño near Santa Ana square.

WALK 2   REAL COLEGIATA DE SAN ISIDRO

Nearby at calle Toledo No. 43, a smell
of warm wax exudes from **Victor Ortega**
(www.cereriaortega.es), one of the last
remaining *cererías*, or candle-makers.
Their main trade is still in the long white
candles for churches, but you can also
buy smaller, more decorative ones.

From the church, walk up calle
Toledo towards the Plaza Mayor. For
lunch try **El Madroño**, a favourite
for locals and visitors, see ❺. This
restaurant has two locations and

choosing between them is easy as
they are just across the road from
each other. Turning right up calle
Imperial brings you to the seventeenth-
century **Palacio de Santa Cruz**, the
current home to the Ministry of
Foreign Affairs. With its slate turrets
and spires, it is another of the key
buildings of the Habsburg period.

From here, you can stroll back into
the Plaza Mayor, down to the Puerta
del Sol or along to Plaza de Santa Ana.

Plaza Mayor, an architectural symphony of bold but balanced lines

WALK 3
Royal Madrid

There is a lot to see on this walk. As well as the majestic Palacio Real, it takes in two royal convents, the Teatro Real opera house, the splendid Plaza de Oriente square and the Almudena cathedral.

DISTANCE: 5km (3 miles)
TIME: A full day
START: Puerta del Sol
END: Jardines de Sabatini
POINTS TO NOTE: This is an interesting walk even if you do not want to visit all the monuments in one day. If you go to the gardens around the palace at the end, you could combine it with a stroll along the Manzanares River.

In the heart of the main shopping area, we veer off to visit two almost hidden convents founded in the sixteenth and seventeenth centuries by the Habsburg monarchs. They look rather unassuming from the outside, but contain astounding collections of artistic treasures.

Calle Arenal

From the **Puerta del Sol ❶**, walk along calle Arenal, west from the square. Now a pleasant pedestrianised shopping street, back in medieval times a stream flowed through here,

which in the summer would dry out to create a sandy promenade.

On the left at No. 9 is the **Palacio de Gaviria**, where the Marquis of Gaviria, a financier from Seville, used to hold grand parties in the nineteenth century. Queen Isabella II was a regular guest.

Just beyond it, a wooden shack selling second-hand books stands on the corner of the pasadizo de San Ginés, a lane leading to the **Chocolatería San Ginés**, see ❶, a Madrid institution that specialises in thick hot chocolate and *churros* – the perfect place to get the energy needed for this walk.

Back on calle Arenal, next on the left is the **Iglesia de San Ginés** (www.parroquiadesangines.es; free). The church features on the town charter of 1202 but the current structure largely dates from the nineteenth century. There is an **El Greco** painting in the Santísimo Cristo chapel, but this is not always open to the public.

Monasterio de las Descalzas Reales

Turn right off calle Arenal up calle San Martín until you get to the Plaza

Changing of the guards at the Palacio Real

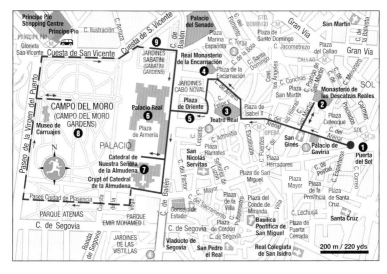

de las Descalzas. Facing you is the long facade of the **Monasterio de las Descalzas Reales ②** (Monastery of the Royal Barefoot Nuns; www.patrimonionacional.es/visita/monasterio-de-las-descalzas-reales; charge, free Wed–Thu 4pm–6.30pm for EU citizens). The convent, where there is still a small community of nuns of the Franciscan order of the Poor Clares, may look rather austere but inside is a secret world that gives a fascinating insight into the Habsburg royal family.

Originally a palace, it was turned into a convent in the mid-sixteenth century by Juana, King Felipe II's sister. The daughters of other royal and aristocratic families joined the order

and a lot of rather valuable donations followed over the years, capturing the richness of Spain's Golden Age. Some of these are now in the Prado Museum, but you can still see Flemish tapestries, frescoes and a great many royal portraits. There are also paintings by El Greco, Titian, Rubens, Velázquez and Zurbarán as well as sculptures by Pedro de Mena and Pompeo de Leoni. From the upper cloister, peep into the inner courtyard where the nuns grow their own vegetables.

Plaza de Isabel II

Return to calle Arenal and continue west to the **Plaza de Isabel II**, originally a space just outside the medieval city

The Monasterio de las Descalzas Reales

Churros & chocolate

Whether for breakfast, in the late afternoon, at the end of a night out or at a street festival, *madrileños* love dipping sugary *churro* fritters into a cup of dense hot chocolate. This is an experience you should definitely try while in the city. Made from just flour, water and salt, *churros* are ridged strips of batter that are piped into huge vats of bubbling oil and fried until golden brown. The strips are then snipped into short lengths with the ends sometimes pressed together to form a loop. Churros must always be consumed as soon as possible as they go stodgy very quickly. The hot chocolate is more like a sauce than a drink and is made from slabs of bitter chocolate melted with cornflour, sugar and milk. Naughty but very nice indeed.

wall where several streams used to merge. Washtubs and bathhouses were set up to take advantage of the water supply, while sandbanks served as a makeshift stage where performances used to take place until a theatre was built in the eighteenth century, which was replaced the following century by the Teatro Real opera house.

Teatro Real

Madrid's grand opera house, the **Teatro Real ❸** (Royal Theatre; www.teatroreal.es/en), stages its own prestigious productions and hosts operas from around the world. You usually need to book online well ahead to get tickets, but the theatre's current success belies its rather rocky history.

Construction began in 1818, but the first performance didn't take place until 1850 as the gigantic theatre was plagued by structural problems, caused by an underground stream and a lack of funds. Following damage during the Civil War and several periods of closure, it reopened in 1997 after lavish refurbishment as a state-of-the-art venue.

Real Monasterio de la Encarnación

Walk up calle Arrieta, along the north side of the opera house, to the tranquil Plaza de la Encarnación. The **Real Monasterio de la Encarnación ❹** (Royal Monastery of the Incarnation; www.patrimonionacional.es) was founded in 1611 by Queen Margarita de Austria, the wife of King Felipe III, and is still home to a few Augustinian nuns.

Designed by Juan Gómez de Mora and Fray Alberto de la Madre de Dios, it contains paintings by leading artists including Vicente Carducho and José de Ribera. The elegant church was restored in the mid-eighteenth century by Ventura Rodríguez, who added marble from various regions of Spain.

It is worth visiting just to see the extraordinary reliquary room, with a

The stately Plaza de Oriente and the Teatro Real

coffered ceiling, which is filled with 1,500 relics in glass and mahogany cases. The most intriguing exhibit is a vial containing what is purported to be the blood of Pantaleon, the doctor saint, which mysteriously liquefies and turns bright red on his feast day, July 27. *Madrileños* queue around the block to see the miracle for themselves and only in years of great crisis does the phenomenon fail to occur.

Plaza de Oriente

On leaving the convent, walk through the gardens opposite, which are part of the vast **Plaza de Oriente** ❺. Or if you are ready for lunch, one of Madrid's most traditional restaurants, **La Bola**, see ❷, is nearby.

The space was initially laid out during the reign of Napoleon's brother, Joseph Bonaparte, king of Spain from 1808–13 during the French occupation. Construction was still underway in the mid-nineteenth century, when the bronze equestrian statue of **Felipe IV** was installed. Designed by Pedro Tacca and based on a painting by Velázquez, the statue was made in 1639 with the help of the Italian scientist Galileo Galilei, who solved the difficulties presented by a horse rearing up on its back legs by making it hollow in front and solid at the back to prevent it from toppling over.

The other statues in the square – of Visigoth leaders and Christian monarchs – were made to adorn the parapet of

the palace but never made it up there. The official reason was that the building could not support their weight or they might fall off. It is also claimed, however, that Isabel de Farnese, Felipe V's second wife, refused to allow their elevation after she had a nightmare in which they crashed down on top of her.

The French influence is reinforced by the lead mansard roofs, stuccoed facades and wrought-iron balconies of the elegant buildings flanking the square. The stylish **Café de Oriente**, see ❸, on the ground floor of one of these buildings, is a comfortable place to rest your feet.

Palacio Real

The name *Oriente* refers to the eastern side of the massive **Palacio Real** ❻ (Royal Palace; www. patrimonionacional.es), standing on the other side of the space.

The Palacio Real is used only for official ceremonies and events (when it is closed to the public).

It stands on the site of the Alcázar, the fortress built by the Moors in the ninth century on a ridge above the Manzanares River. The strategic location, with panoramic views across the countryside, was an ideal lookout.

When the Alcázar burned down on Christmas Eve 1734, it gave King Felipe V (the first Bourbon king of Spain) the opportunity to replace it with a magnificent stone and granite structure along French-Italian lines.

The original architect, Felipe Juvarra, planned a building twice the size, but he died in 1739 and his student Giovanni Battista Sacchetti took over.

Be prepared for a visual onslaught inside, as the ornate decoration bombards your senses at every turn. The endless lavish rooms include the **throne room**, where Tiepolo painted the ceiling with an allegory of the Majesty of Spain. The **Gasparini room**, with embroidered silver silk covering the walls and a swirling marble mosaic floor, was restored in the 1990s but has otherwise remained practically unchanged since the time Carlos III used it. He was the first king to live there in 1764, the last was Alfonso XIII, who left when he abdicated the throne in 1931. After a long period with no royals in Spain, the seventeenth-century Zarzuela Palace northwest of the city became residence for Prince Juan Carlos and his family in 1963. Today's monarchs, King Felipe VI and Queen Letizia, live in a smaller palace built in the same complex in 2002.

The **Galeria de las Colecciones Reales** (www.galeriadelas coleccionesreales.es; charge), a new addition, opened in June 2023. The museum shows at least some of the royal collections stored for lack of space, organized by dynasties (Trastámara, Hapsburg and Bourbon), with a description of each ruler showing possessions from each monarch's period. The collections include tapestries, paintings, clothing, furniture, several carriages, and a lot more. There is a small archeological section, showing part of the foundation of the Islamic fortress discovered during construction of the museum, and a large area for temporary exhibits.

Even if you do not visit the Galeria, be sure to visit the lookout between the Palace and the Cathedral, the perfect place to understand the strategic value of the Islamic fortress: there's a great view over the **Casa de Campo Park** to the west and on a clear day out to the **Guadarrama mountains** to the north. This is also a good place to watch the sunset.

Catedral de Nuestra Señora de la Almudena

On the opposite side of the square is the **Catedral de Nuestra Señora de la Almudena** ❼ (www.catedraldela almudena.es; free). Begun in the nineteenth century but not finished until 1993, it combines a variety of styles, with the neo-Gothic interior contained within a neoclassical shell, devised by Fernando Chueca Goitia and Carlos Sidro in the 1940s. Inside, light streams in through rose windows and the dome crowns the Latin-cross transept.

Be sure to visit the **crypt on Cuesta de la Vega** to see the neo-Romanesque capitals, stained-glass windows and the figure of the Virgin of the Almudena.

The lavish dining room in the Palacio Real

Food and drink

1 Chocolatería San Ginés
Pasadizo de San Ginés 5;
https://chocolateriasangines.com; €
In business since 1894, this is the
most well-known place to indulge
in churros with hot chocolate.

2 La Bola
Calle La Bola 5; https://labola.es; €€
Pretty restaurant with a red frontage
founded in 1870 that specialises
in traditional *madrileño* dishes,
particularly *cocido madrileño* stew.

3 Café de Oriente
Plaza de Oriente 2;
www.cafedeoriente.es; €€
The brick-vaulted restaurant serves
traditional dishes such as braised
beef cheeks in red wine, while the café
has tapas, sandwiches and burgers.

4 El Ventorrillo
Calle Bailén 14, Las Vistillas;
tel: 91 366 3578; €€
One of the most romantic spots in
the city. You might end up staying for
hours, ordering a plate of prawns
while watching the sun go down.

Cross the road when you come out of the crypt to see vestiges of the walls built by Moors in the ninth century and Christians in the twelfth century. As the road bends sharply to the left, you can see foundations of the Vega Gate, west entrance to the Muslim fortress-city and the first line of Christian walls. Just south of the walls is the **Parque Emir Mohammed I**, which is sometimes used for concerts during the summer.

The palace gardens
If you still have energy left at this point, you can stroll around the palace gardens. Continue down the hill through the Parque de Atenas, then turn right along the Paseo de la Vírgen del Puerto to the entrance of the **Campo del Moro** 8 gardens. For centuries the steep escarpment was an effective natural defence.

Turn right when you come out, then skirt the gardens by turning right again up the Cuesta de San Vicente until you come to the staircase up to the **Sabatini** 9 gardens on the north side of the palace. If you don't want to climb the hill up to the gardens, cross Cuesta de San Vicente and take the metro at the Principe Pio stop directly to Opera on the shuttle "R" line.

If you don't fancy such a trek when you come out of the crypt cross the viaduct over the calle Segovia to get to the shady **El Ventorrillo** terrace, see 4, where you can sit and enjoy a refreshing drink, and perhaps stay for the sunset.

Sunset over the Catedral and Palacio Real

WALK 4
The Paseo del Prado

This walk explores the top half of the Paseo del Prado and the elegant streets of the Jerónimos district, taking in the impressive Museo Nacional Thyssen-Bornemisza.

WALK 4   THE PASEO DEL PRADO

> **DISTANCE:** 1.5km (1 mile)
> **TIME:** Half a day
> **START:** Plaza de Cibeles
> **END:** Plaza de Neptuno
> **POINTS TO NOTE:** Although the walk is short, visiting the museums takes time so do bear that in mind. Afterwards, you could go to the Retiro Park (walk 6) or the Barrio de Las Letras (walk 7). The Paseo del Prado, Jeronimos district and Retiro Park form a World Heritage site under the name "Paseo del Prado and Buen Retiro, a landscape of Arts and Sciences".

Madrid's major museums are situated along the Paseo del Prado, also known as the Paseo del Arte – the Art Walk. The lower section, where the Prado and Reina Sofía museums are situated, is explored separately in walk 5, as it can be exhausting and overwhelming to visit them all on the same day.

Plaza de Cibeles

Traffic streams at all hours of the day and night around the **Plaza de Cibeles ❶**, which connects the key parts of the city. In the centre of the square, the **Fuente de Cibeles** is one of Madrid's main landmarks. The fountain features Cybele, the goddess of nature, in a chariot pulled by two lions. A symbol of the fertility of the land around the city, the fountain is where fans of Real Madrid football club converge after important victories.

Occupying a huge block on the corner of calle de Alcalá and the Paseo del Prado is the **Banco de España** (Bank of Spain), with a magnificent entrance decorated with sculptures by Jerónimo Suñol. Across calle de Alcalá, on the northwest corner, is the **Palacio de Buenavista**, built for the Duchess of Alba in the eighteenth century and now the headquarters of the Spanish army. On calle de Alcalá between the two buildings is the eternal flame in memory of victims of the COVID virus, especially lethal in Spain in 2020.

The neo-Baroque **Palacio de Linares** takes up the northeast corner. Built in the late nineteenth century for the Marquis of Linares, the palace has sumptuous interiors and is said

Strolling down the Paseo del Prado's shady boulevard

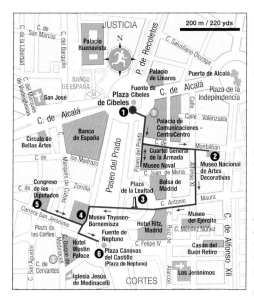

CentroCentro (http://centrocentro.org; free), where there are usually a few exhibitions on. It is worth going in just to see the elaborate interior. Zoom up to the observation deck for panoramic views across the city. If your knees allow it, from the deck walk down the stairs at the front of the building to appreciate the fabulous architecture of this building. You can also have a drink in the chic terrace **bar**, see ❶, on the sixth floor (open from 1pm).

Paseo del Prado

The Plaza de Cibeles marks the start of the **Paseo del Prado**, laid out during the Enlightenment period. The northern section of the boulevard, down to Plaza de Neptuno, was devoted to leisure – a place to walk and parade around in carriages – while the lower half (see walk 5) was more about education, science and medicine.

On the left at No. 5, it is easy to miss the **Museo Naval** (www.armada.mde.es/museonaval), where highlights include a map drawn up in 1500 by Juan de la Cosa, which was the first to show the territories of the New World. Walk up calle Montalbán to see the

to be haunted (www.esmadrid.com/informacion-turistica/palacio-del-marques-de-linares). Also in the building is the **Casa de América** (www.casamerica.es; free), a Latin American cultural centre with a lively programme of exhibitions, concerts and talks.

Palacio de Comunicaciones

Dominating the square is the curving white **Palacio de Comunicaciones**, the gloriously ornate former main post office designed by Antonio Palacios, the man behind several of Madrid's grandest buildings of the early twentieth century. It is now the City Hall and also houses

The Fuente de Cibeles and the Palacio de Comunicaciones

main part of the building, the **Cuartel General de la Armada**, headquarters of the Spanish Navy Ministry, with an elaborate facade featuring Portuguese Manueline decoration.

Museo Nacional de Artes Decorativas

At the top of calle Montalbán at No. 12 is the **Museo Nacional de Artes Decorativas ❷** (www.cultura. gob.es/mnartesdecorativas/portada. html), housed in a grand nineteenth-century palace. The excellent displays include tapestries, leatherwork, ceramics, jewellery, fans and furniture, as well as an eighteenth-century Valencian kitchen.

Turn left out of the museum, then left again along the tree-lined calle Alfonso XI and take the second right down the broad calle Antonio Maura. This is the elegant Jerónimos area, with red-brick apartment buildings with wrought-iron mirador balconies. You might recognise the streets from Pedro Almodóvar's 1988 film *Women on the Verge of a Nervous Breakdown*.

Plaza de la Lealtad

Calle Antonio Maura leads to the **Plaza de la Lealtad ❸**, where an obelisk marks the centre of the **Monumento a los Caídos por España**, a cenotaph built for those who died in Madrid's battle against French troops on May 2, 1808. It now also honours all those who have given their lives for Spain.

On the right of the square is the **Bolsa de Comercio** (www.bolsamadrid. es; visits by appointment only). Built in the late nineteenth century, Madrid's stock exchange has a concave, arcaded facade that makes the triangular site look much bigger than it actually is.

On the opposite side of the square is the **Mandarin Oriental Ritz** (see page 94), built in 1908 by the French architect Charles Mewes, who had previously designed the *Ritz* hotels in Paris and London.

Museo Nacional Thyssen-Bornemisza

Cross the Paseo del Prado to reach the **Museo Nacional Thyssen-Bornemisza ❹** (www.museothyssen.org; charge). The superlative displays of art from the thirteenth to the twentieth centuries were built up by Baron Heinrich Thyssen-Bornemisza and extended by his son, Hans Heinrich, who died in 2002. Considered to be one of the best collections in the world, around 1,000 artworks are on show in the Palacio de Villahermosa, a handsome neoclassical structure that was remodelled to house the museum by Rafael Moneo.

Visiting the Museo Nacional Thyssen-Bornemisza

Divided into Old Masters and New Masters, the displays are arranged over three floors, in chronological order, starting at the top of the building. The baron's widow, Carmen Thyssen-

Lichtenstein at the Thyssen-Bornemisza

Bornemisza, has overseen the museum since his death and her own prestigious collection is displayed in a wing added in 2004, with paintings by Gauguin, Van Gogh, Braque and Picasso.

On the second floor, **Level 2**, masterpieces include Domenico Ghirlandaio's *Portrait of Goivanna Tornabuoni* (1488), Hans Holbein the Younger's *Portrait of Henry VIII* and *Jesus among the Doctors* by Albrecht Dürer.

On **Level 1**, highlights include *Woman with a Parasol* by Pierre-Auguste Renoir, *Swaying Dancer* by Edgar Degas, *Metropolis* by George Grosz, *Seated Woman* by Juan Gris and *Hotel Room* by Edward Hopper. The displays continue on **Level 0**, the ground floor, with works by Salvador Dalí and Roy Lichtenstein.

Congreso de los Diputados

Turn right out of the museum and right again up Carrera de San Jerónimo. On the right is the **Congreso de los Diputados** ❺ (www.congreso.es/en/home). More commonly known as **Las Cortes**, the seat of the Spanish Parliament (1842–50) has a neoclassical portico guarded by lions, which were cast using bronze from cannons seized during the African war of 1860.

Opposite is the triangular **Plaza de las Cortes**, with a statue of Miguel de Cervantes marking the entrance to the Barrio de Las Letras (see walk 7). On the southwest corner of the square is the Parisian-style **Hotel Westin Palace** (see page 94), which opened in 1912

and has always been a favourite haunt of artists and writers, including Dalí and Picasso. You can enjoy a drink under the stained-glass dome in the sumptuous Rotonda lounge, or for a beer and a tapa in a more down to earth setting, head for **Taberna El Rincón de José**, see ❷, around the corner.

Marking the end of this part of the Paseo del Prado is the **Plaza de Neptuno** ❻. The marble **Fuente de Neptuno** in the centre features Neptune, god of the sea, holding a trident and standing on a shell-shaped chariot drawn by seahorses.

Frank Marc's artwork at the Thyssen-Bornemisza

Under the Hotel Westin dome

WALK 5
The Prado and Reina Sofía museums

Many people go to Madrid just to visit the Prado, but there is a lot more to see on the Paseo del Prado, however, with contemporary art at the Reina Sofía and CaixaForum museums, and the tranquil Royal Botanic Garden for relaxing in between.

DISTANCE: 1km (0.6 mile)
TIME: A full day
START: Museo del Prado
END: Museo Nacional de Arte Contemporáneo Reina Sofía
POINTS TO NOTE: The overall distance covered will of course depend on how many museums you visit. You could combine it with walks 6 or 7. The Paseo del Prado, Jeronimos district and Retiro Park form a World Heritage site under the name "Paseo del Prado and Buen Retiro, a landscape of Arts and Sciences". The Prado Museum opens now and then at night. See dates on the website.

This stretch of the Paseo del Prado more than lives up to its alternative name as the Paseo del Arte (Art Walk). Allow as much time as possible to enjoy not only visiting the museums but also taking in the spirit of the boulevard itself, which was created to improve the quality of life for the *madrileños*.

The Museo del Prado

The **Museo del Prado** ❶ (www.museo delprado.es; charge) is one of the greatest museums in the world and you could spend days contemplating its astounding displays. As well as works by Spanish masters such as El Greco, Velázquez and Goya, there are wonderful Italian and Flemish collections with paintings by Raphael, Titian, Tintoretto, Bosch and Rubens, alongside some temporary exhibitions as well.

Designed by Juan de Villanueva in 1785, the neoclassical building was originally intended to be a natural history museum, part of Carlos III's grand plan for the Paseo del Prado as a place of learning and leisure. It was not until the reign of Fernando VII (1814–33) that the building was used to house the royal collections of art, with the museum opening in 1819.

At the beginning of the twenty-first century, Pritzker prize-winning architect Rafael Monco designed a new section linking the main structure to the cloister of the Jerónimos church behind the building. Used

The Museo del Prado, fronted by a statue of Diego Velázquez

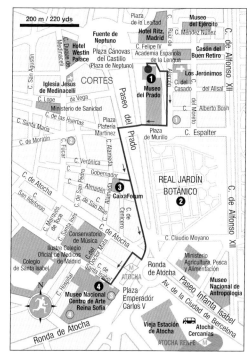

about 10 percent of its collections.

Visiting the Prado

Most visitors only have a few hours to spend in the museum, so it is advisable to decide what you most want to see. You might want to concentrate on the Velázquez, Goya and Bosch paintings. That said, even the best of intentions are likely to go astray as you stroll through the halls, given the quality and quantity of work on display, and just wandering around making your own discoveries has a lot to be said for it too.

Access to the museum is at the north end of the building – the Goya entrance or the Jerónomos entrance. You usually have to queue to buy tickets, so if possible, save time by pre-booking online. Audio-guides are available.

for temporary exhibitions, it features sculptural doors by Cristina Iglesias.

The Prado's collections were commissioned and acquired by Spain's monarchs over the centuries and reflect their links with other countries as well as their personal tastes. The museum also received substantial holdings following the disentailment of religious property in the nineteenth century. Although the museum is vast, the Prado only displays

Spanish collections

The Prado's unsurpassable Spanish paintings begin with Romanesque art and end with Goya. Masterpieces from the twelfth to the sixteenth centuries include works by Bartolomé

Admiring the masterpieces in the Museo del Prado

Bermejo, Juan de Juanes and Pedro Berruguete. The seventeenth-century displays are particularly impressive, with paintings by José de Ribera, Murillo and Zurbarán.

El Greco

Domenikos Theotokopoulos (1541–1614), known as El Greco (The Greek), was born in Crete and lived in Toledo from 1577 until his death, working on his dramatic canvases that feature ethereal elongated figures in hues of grey, mauve and yellow. *The Nobleman with his Hand on his Chest*, restored in the 1990s, is one of the earliest he painted in Spain. One of his last works was *The Adoration of the Shepherds*, which he painted for his own burial chapel.

Velázquez

The paintings by Diego de Velázquez (1599–1660) are in the centre of the first floor. *Las Meninas* (*The Maids of Honour* or *The Family of Philip IV*), which many experts consider to be the greatest work of Western art, is in the oval room at the heart of the museum. Painted in 1656, this is the work that attracts the greatest crowds. Everyone is captivated by this puzzle of a picture, in which Velázquez portrayed himself, perhaps painting the king and queen, who are reflected in a mirror, watched by their daughter the Infanta Margarita, her maids of honour and other court figures. The role of each character in

the painting and what they represent has intrigued both art historians and the casual viewer for centuries.

The Surrender of Breda depicts the triumph of the Spanish over the Dutch at the Siege of Breda in 1625, with the victor humbly accepting the key to the town. In *The Triumph of Bacchus* (better known as *The Topers* or *The Drunkards*) and the later work *The Spinners* (also known as *The Fable of Arachne*), he painted mythological figures as everyday characters.

Goya

Goya's works are at the southern end on the ground, first and second floors. Francisco de Goya (1746–1828) was court artist to Carlos IV and painted numerous royal portraits. In *Carlos IV and his Family* (1800), he pays tribute to Velázquez by painting himself in the left-hand corner; the king has an absentminded look and the queen has beady eyes. Two of his most powerful paintings, *The Second of May, 1808, in Madrid: the Charge of the Mamelukes*, and *The Third of May, 1808, in Madrid: The Executions at Príncipe Pío*, commemorate the desperate, unsuccessful attempts to prevent the city falling under French control.

Goya's nightmarish *Black Paintings* were created at the end of his life, originally painted on the walls of his house by the Manzanares River. On the second floor are the cartoons he painted for the Royal Tapestry

The Triumph of Bacchus (1628–29), by Velázquez

Factory (see page 57), depicting typical scenes and local festivals.

Flemish, German and Dutch collections

The rich collections include Rogier van der Weyden's great masterpiece, *Descent from the Cross*, which Felipe II inherited from his aunt, Mary of Hungary, and Self-Portrait at 26 by Albrecht Dürer (1471–1528).

King Felipe II was fascinated by the work of Hieronymous Bosch (1450–1516) and had several of his best works at his monastery-palace at El Escorial (see page 82). *The Haywain* is inspired by the Flemish proverb: "The world is a haywain from which every man takes what he can." His most famous creation, *The Garden of Earthly Delights* (*c.*1505) shows mankind engaged in ephemeral pleasures in the central panel, with Paradise on the left and Hell on the right.

Only a handful of the Prado's extensive holdings of paintings by Peter Paul Rubens (1577–1640) are on display, but these include *The Adoration of the Magi* and *The Three Graces*, which features the faces of both the artist's wives.

Italian collections

Among the superlative early Italian works, which came mainly from the royal collections, are *The Story of Nastagio degli Onesti* panels by Sandro Botticelli (1445–1510)

and the delicate *Annunciation* by Fra Angelico (circa 1400–55).

The identity of the sitter in the magnificent *Portrait of a Cardinal* (1510) by Raphael (1483-1520) has never been discovered. Titian, who worked for both Carlos V and Felipe II, painted *The Emperor Charles V in Mühlberg* following the battle in 1547 when the emperor triumphed over the Protestants. Among the paintings by Tintoretto (1518–94) is *Christ Washing the Disciples' Feet,* which is a superb example of his extraordinary skill at perspective.

You probably need a break when you emerge from the Prado. There is a pleasant terrace café by the exit, or you could walk up the steps on the right to calle Ruiz de Alarcón, then right along the street to the **Murillo Café**, see ❶.

When you have recovered, turn left out of the café and immediately right into the **Plaza de Murillo**, at the southern end of the Prado building, where there are fountains of children playing with dolphins, designed by Ventura Rodríguez in 1781.

Real Jardín Botánico

On the left of the square is the peaceful **Real Jardín Botánico** ❷ (www.rjb.csic.es; charge), a great oasis in which to spend a quiet hour between museums.

At the entrance, look at the neoclassical gate, the Puerta de Murillo, designed by Juan de Villanueva. Founded in the eighteenth

The much-admired Garden of Earthly Delights (c.1505), by Bosch

century, the garden was originally devised by the botanist Casimiro Gómez Ortega to cultivate the plants brought back from Spanish colonies all around the world. Back then, the Reina Sofía museum just down the road was a hospital, so the idea was to provide a supply of plants for medicinal purposes.

Old varieties of rose flank the Paseo de Carlos III, which leads down to the Puerta Real, a gate designed by Sabatini. On the second level, look out for the elm tree known as *Pantalones*, because the trunk is divided into two and it looks like a pair of trousers. There is an oval pond on the upper level, surrounded by trees including a Canarian palm. The pavilion at the back was originally a hothouse but is now used for temporary exhibitions.

Cross the Paseo del Prado. If you are ready for lunch, there are lots of good places around the Plaza Platería Martínez, such as **Vinoteca Moratín**, see ❷.

CaixaForum

Continuing down the Paseo del Prado, on the right at No. 36 you reach the **CaixaForum** cultural centre ❸ (https://caixaforum.org/es/madrid). Originally an electrical power plant dating back to the early twentieth century, it was remodelled in 2008 by the Swiss architects Herzog & de Meuron, who added a galvanised steel outer casing and a vertical garden. Inside, the seven floors are linked by a dramatic white concrete staircase. As well as temporary exhibitions, there is a varied programme of concerts, talks and other activities.

Walk down the last block of the Paseo del Prado to reach the Glorieta de Atocha crossroads (official name Plaza del Emperador Carlos V), and cross over calle Atocha to the Reina Sofía museum on Plaza de Santa Isabel.

Museo Nacional Centro de Arte Reina Sofía

The **Museo Nacional Centro de Arte Reina Sofía** ❹ (www.museoreinasofia.es; charge) is Madrid's enormous museum of contemporary art, where there are usually a few major temporary exhibitions underway, and the extensive permanent collection.

Pablo Picasso's great masterpiece *Guernica* draws the biggest crowds but there is a lot more to see, including superlative works by Salvador Dalí, Joan Miró and Antoni Tàpies. International artists include Georges Braque, Julian Schnabel and Richard Serra. The museum is housed in the eighteenth-century Hospital General de San Carlos, with a new section designed by French architect Jean Nouvel.

Visiting the Reina Sofía

It is easy to spend all day in this museum – accessed via glass lifts on the outside of the structure. Luckily, there are two great places to eat, drink and rest: **Arzábal** ❸ and **NuBel** ❹,

The vertical garden at CaixaForum

Food and drink

1 Murillo Café

Calle Ruiz de Alarcón 27;
www.murillocafe.com; €€
An attractive café with terrace tables,
where you can stop for breakfast, coffee,
brunch or lunch. There is a range of
fresh juices, salads and tasty pizzas.

2 Vinoteca Moratín

Calle Moratín 36;
www.vinotecamoratin.com; €€
Modern Spanish food with a seasonal
menu and excellent Spanish and
international wines in a relaxed
bistro setting. One of the best places
in the area for lunch or dinner,
with reasonable prices too.

3 Arzábal

Museo Reina Sofía;
www.arzabal.com; €€
Try contemporary Spanish tapas and
full meals from chef Iván Morales,
or just have a drink as there are bar
and restaurant areas with indoor and
outdoor tables. The terrace is lovely
for a romantic dinner. If you are not
in the museum, there is also access
from the street on Ronda de Atocha.

4 NuBel

Museo Reina Sofía; www.nubel.es; €€
Everything from breakfast to burgers,
coffee to cocktails is available in this
futuristic space in the Nouvel wing of
the Reina Sofía museum, which will
thrill fans of contemporary design.

both with outdoor tables, as well as
a good shop for books and gifts.

The work is displayed chronologically,
starting on Level 2, which covers
1900–45. Among the paintings by
Salvador Dalí are *Girl at the Window*
and *Face of the Great Masturbator*.

Guernica

Pablo Picasso (1881–1973) painted
his masterpiece for the Spanish
Pavilion of the 1937 Paris World Fair,
in response to the bombing earlier
that year of the town of Guernica
in the Basque Country by German
planes on the orders of General
Franco. The painting has come to
symbolise universal suffering and
the savagery of war. Although most
people are familiar with the image,
the emotional impact of seeing the
original is often overwhelming.

The displays continue on Level 3,
spanning the period 1945–68, with
works by Antoni Tàpies, Eduardo
Chillida, Antonio López and Antonio
Saura. Level 4 is used for temporary
exhibitions and the permanent
collections continue on Level 1, the
ground floor, where highlights from
1962 to 1982 include sculptures by
Richard Serra and Juan Muñoz.

Lichtenstein outside the Reina Sofía Museum

CaixaForum's staircase

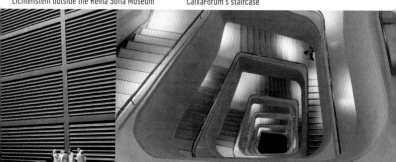

WALK 6
The Retiro Park and Atocha

The *madrileños* are fond of their main park, particularly on Sunday mornings, when families come to stroll around and sit at the many outdoor cafés. It is well worth exploring the area to the south too, where there are a few lesser-known sights.

DISTANCE: 4km (2.5 miles)
TIME: Three hours
START: Puerta de Alcalá
END: Real Fábrica de Tapices
POINTS TO NOTE: This is a good walk to do after a morning at one of the major museums. It is intended to give you an idea of the layout of the Retiro Park, rather than to be followed exactly. The Paseo del Prado, Jeronimos district and Retiro Park form a World Heritage Site, under the name "Paseo del Prado and Buen Retiro, a landscape of Arts and Sciences".

There's always a lot going on in the Retiro, where people come to jog, row boats, see puppet shows, or just read at a café terrace. South is Atocha train station, with the fascinating Royal Tapestry Factory nearby.

Puerta de Alcalá

Dominating the circular Plaza de la Independencia, by the main entrance to the park, is the **Puerta de Alcalá ❶** (Alcalá Gate), a triumphal arch built for Carlos III by Francesco Sabatini in the late eighteenth century and one of Madrid's most important symbols.

For a quick breakfast or sandwiches for a picnic, pop into **Rodilla**, see ❶, before going into the park.

Parque del Buen Retiro

The northeast corner of the Plaza de la Independencia leads to the **Parque del Buen Retiro** (Retiro Park).

The rectangular park has evolved from its origins in the seventeenth century as the gardens of the Palacio del Buen Retiro, which was built for Felipe IV. This was a huge complex on the hill behind the Prado, but only the ballroom and one wing have survived. The Retiro became a public park in 1868.

From the entrance, Avenida Méjico leads up diagonally to the lake, one of the few surviving elements from the old palace. Back in the seventeenth century, it was used for extravagant theatrical performances or naval battles. Now it's only rowing boats causing

Monument to Alfonso XII and the boating lake

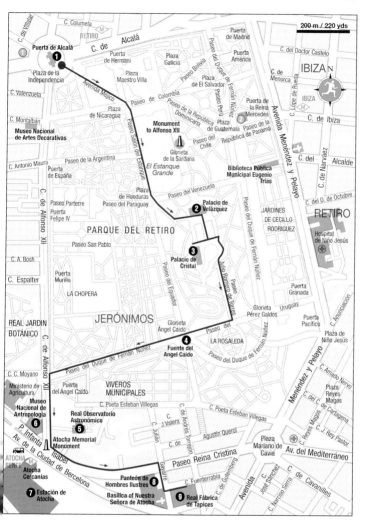

Puerta de Alcalá ➊

C. Columela
RETIRO
C. de Alcalá
Puerta
de Madrid
Puerta
de Hermani
Plaza
Galicia
Puerta
América
IBIZA N
C. de
Menorca
Plaza de la
Independencia
Avenida Méjico
Plaza
Maestro Villa
C. de Ibiza
IBIZA
Puerta de
la Reina
Mercedes
C. Valenzuela
Paseo de Colombia
C. Montalbán
Plaza
de Nicaragua
Museo Nacional
de Artes Decorativas
Monument
to Alfonso XII
Plaza
de Guatemala
Paseo de la
República de Panamá
C. de Ibiza
Glorieta
de la Sardana
Paseo del
Chile
C. Antonio Maura
Puerta
de España
Paseo de la Argentina
El Estanque
Grande
Biblioteca Pública
Municipal Eugenio
Trías
C. del Narváez
RETIRO
Paseo Parterre
Plaza
de Honduras
Paseo del Paraguay
Paseo del Venezuela
Palacio de
Velázquez ➋
JARDINES
DE CECILIO
RODRÍGUEZ
C. del D. de Octubre
Hospital
de Niño Jesús
PARQUE DEL RETIRO
Paseo San Pablo
Palacio de
Cristal ➌
Puerta
Granada
C. A. Bosh
Puerta
Murillo
LA CHOPERA
JERÓNIMOS
Glorieta
Ángel Caído
Glorieta
Pérez Galdós
Uruguay
Puerta
Pacífico
REAL JARDIN
BOTÁNICO
Fuente del
Angel Caído ➍
LA ROSALEDA
Plaza de
Niño Jesús
C. C. Moyano
Puerta
del Ángel Caído
VIVEROS
MUNICIPALES
Paseo del Duque de Fernán Núñez
Ministerio de
Agricultura
Museo
Nacional de
Antropología ➏
Real Observatorio
Astronómico ➎
Plaza
Reyes
Magos
ATOCHA
RENFE
Atocha Memorial
Monument
Plaza
Mariano de
Cavia
Av. del Mediterráneo
Atocha
Cercanías
Estación de
Atocha ➐
Paseo Reina Cristina
Panteón de
Hombres Ilustres ➑
Basílica of Nuestra
Señora de Atocha
Real Fábrica
de Tapices ➒

200 m / 220 yds

Music in the Retiro Park   Fountain in the park

Visiting the bullring

You can visit Madrid's bullring and its museum without actually seeing a bullfight. Leave the Retiro Park a little east of Plaza de la Independencia and jump on the metro at Retiro stop (line 2) straight to Ventas station, emerging at the **Plaza de Toros de Las Ventas** (Las Ventas Bullring; www.las-ventas.com). The arena, inaugurated in 1934, is the biggest in Spain with a diameter of 60 metres (197 ft) and room for 24,000 spectators. The **Museo Taurino** (Bullfighting Museum; https://lasventastour.com/en) provides a good overview of what bullfighting is all about with a tour taking in the Mexican-style chapel where the bullfighters pray before the fight, the surgery and the suits of lights worn by famous matadors, along with their capes and swords.

ripples in the water (available for hire). Presiding over it is the semicircular **Monumento a Alfonso XII**, designed by José Grases Riera in 1922.

Turn right and walk along the promenade flanking the lake. At the end, bear diagonally left to reach the **Palacio de Velázquez** ❷, a large pavilion built in the late nineteenth century now used for exhibitions staged by the Reina Sofía museum (see page 52). Adjacent, overlooking a smaller lake, the **Palacio de Cristal** ❸, was built around the same time and is also now an exhibition venue. A superb example of iron and glass architecture, it was inspired by London's Crystal Palace and the Palm House at Kew Gardens.

Continuing south, you reach the broad Paseo de Uruguay. Opposite is the **Rosaleda**, a rose garden. Perhaps the most intriguing of the many fountains in the park is the **Fuente del Ángel Caído** ❹ (Fallen Angel Fountain), standing where the Paseo de Uruguay meets the Paseo de Cuba. Made by Ricardo Bellver in 1878, it represents Lucifer's descent to Hell and is one of the few statues in the world that celebrate the devil. Madrid lore claims the fountain's altitude is exactly 666 metres.

There are lots of cafés dotted around the park, but the most attractive is **Florida Retiro**, see ❷, a pavilion on the eastern edge behind the lake.

To explore beyond the park, from the Ángel Caído fountain, continue down the Paseo del Fernán Nuñez. Just west of the Ángel Caído on your left there is a reconstruction of a waterwheel. Several of these existed in the park for irrigation, this one also supplied water for the Royal Porcelain Factory, on this site from 1760 until its destruction in 1812 during the Peninsular War.

Continue downhill to the park exit on calle Algonso XII. Turning left out of the park, immediately on the left is the **Real Observatorio Astronómico** ❺ (www.ign.es; charge). You must book ahead to visit the observatory,

The exquisite Palacio de Cristal

a superb neoclassical structure designed by Juan de Villanueva.

Continuing down calle Alfonso XII, the grandiose building with ceramic decoration on the right is the **Ministerio de Agricultura** (Ministry of Agriculture).

Museo Nacional de Antropología

The neoclassical structure at the bottom of the hill is the **Museo Nacional de Antropología** 🟠 (www.cultura.gob.es; charge). Displays include Tuareg and Berber exhibits from North Africa and mummies of Guanches, the original inhabitants of the Canary Islands.

Around Atocha

Opposite the museum is the **Estación de Atocha** 🟠 (Atocha Station). The circular red-brick entrance designed by Rafael Moneo in 1992 adjoins the old ironwork station, which has been turned into a hothouse of palm trees.

Walk east along the Paseo de la Infanta Isabel to the corner of calle Julián Gayarre. The belltower belongs to the **Pantheon of Spain** 🟠 (www.patrimonionacional.es; free), previously the Panteón de Hombres Ilustres, home to elaborate tombs of politicians, writers, artists and military men.

The pantheon occupies the cloister of the neo-Baroque **Basílica de Nuestra Señora de Atocha** (Basilica of Our Lady of Atocha; free). The Virgin of Atocha is much revered in Madrid.

Food and drink

🔴 Rodilla
Calle de Alcalá 67; www.rodilla.es; €
There are branches all over town of this handy, reasonably priced sandwich shop, which has been going since 1939. There is a wide range of sandwiches, and you can eat in or take away.

🔴 Florida Retiro
Paseo República de Panamá, Parque del Retiro; www.floridaretiro.com; €€
Sit down for a drink, snack or meal in this attractive conservatory-style gastrobar and restaurant. The mozzarella, mortadella and truffle toasted sandwich is good with a beer. There are evening shows in an adjoining venue.

Real Fábrica de Tapices

Opposite at calle Fuenterrabía No. 2, a slim chimney rises from the brick and rubblework building of the **Real Fábrica de Tapices** 🟠 (Royal Tapestry Factory; www.realfabricadetapices.com; charge). It has been on this site since the end of the nineteenth century but was founded in 1720 by Felipe V.

Turning right and then right again from the factory brings you to the Avenida de la Ciudad de Barcelona, where you can take the metro from Menéndez Pelayo station back to Puerta del Sol.

The luxuriant Estación de Atocha

WALK 7
Plaza de Santa Ana and the Barrio de Las Letras

The characterful area around Plaza de Santa Ana, known as the Barrio de Las Letras – the Literary Quarter – was where Madrid's first theatres emerged at the end of the sixteenth century. A vibrant, arty vibe pervades the streets to this day.

TIME: Two hours
DISTANCE: 2km (1.25 miles)
START/END: Plaza de Santa Ana
POINTS TO NOTE: It is fun to do this walk in the early evening, maybe after the Thyssen-Bornemisza or Prado museums, stopping off at tapas bars.

The area is now full of bars and independent boutiques, but for centuries poets, playwrights and novelists lived in this triangle of narrow streets. Although not much survives from Spain's Golden Age in the seventeenth century, as you walk around it is easy to imagine the intrigues that took place here.

Plaza de Santa Ana

The focal point of the neighbourhood, the **Plaza de Santa Ana** ❶ was created when a large convent was demolished in the nineteenth century. Dominating the square at the eastern end is the neoclassical **Teatro Español**, Madrid's most important theatre. It has evolved into this grand building from its origins as the Corral del Príncipe, a simple wooden playhouse, where plays by the luminaries of the Golden Age were staged every afternoon. A statue of the poet and playwright Federico García Lorca (1898–1936) in front of the theatre is a popular meeting point.

At the other end of the square, a large marble statue of the renowned playwright Pedro Calderón (1600–81) stands in front of the sparkling white *ME Madrid Reina Victoria* hotel (see page 94). Looking as if it has been transported from a genteel spa resort, with its turret topped with a spherical beacon, it used to be a renowned favourite of bullfighters, particularly Manolete.

The most famous of the many bar on the square is the **Cervecería Alemana** at No. 6, see ❶, where Ernest Hemingway used to meet up with bullfighting friends in the 1950s.

The ME Madrid Reina Victoria hotel dominates the Plaza de Santa Ana

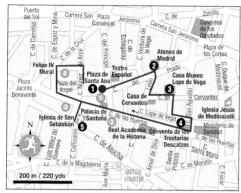

be seen in the sixteenth and seventeenth centuries. Members of the theatrical profession came to strike deals and hire people, but of course the main attraction was the opportunity to pick up on the latest scandals.

Casa Museo Lope de Vega

Walk down calle Cervantes to No. 11, where the home of the great playwright of the Golden Age, Félix Lope de Vega, is now the **Casa Museo Lope de Vega**  (http://casamuseolopedevega.org; charge, book in advance). Lope de Vega lived here from 1610 until his death in 1635 at the age of 73. He is thought to have written 1,500 plays, novels and poetry, drawing on the many dramas, tragedies and passionate affairs in his own life. His works are still frequently performed throughout Spain.

Although very few of the playwright's belongings have survived, the museum is a good recreation of a home of the time; it is austerely decorated with furniture of the period and set around a peaceful courtyard garden. If you are lucky, you might see a Lope-period character wandering the streets nearby.

Across the street from the museum, walk up the short calle Quevedo. A

Calle del Prado

Leave the square at the southeast corner and walk down calle del Prado, where several antique bookshops survive. At No. 21 on the left is the **Ateneo de Madrid** ❷ (www.ateneodemadrid.com), which was founded in 1835 by a group of liberal intellectuals. Although it is a private club, visitors can usually wander in and have a look at the panelled interiors, portrait gallery and library.

Walk back up calle del Prado and turn left into calle León – the name comes from a lion kept in a cage here in the seventeenth century. On the left, on the corner of calle Cervantes, a plaque marks the site of the house where Miguel de Cervantes, Spain's greatest writer and the author of *Don Quixote*, died in 1616.

Another plaque commemorates the *mentidero de representantes*, the spot where the movers and shakers of the theatrical world would meet to see and

plaque on the corner with calle Lope de Vega indicates where the poet and satirist Francisco de Quevedo (1580–1645) once lived, after evicting his arch-rival Luis de Góngora.

Convento de las Trinitarias Descalzas

Opposite, on calle Lope de Vega, is the seventeenth-century **Convento de las Trinitarias Descalzas** ❹ (Convent of the Barefoot Trinitarians). A few nuns still live in the massive convent, which is not open to the public. In the church, a stone tablet commemorates that Cervantes was buried there, although it is unclear whether the tomb is still there or not. Walking down calle Lope de Vega and turning right into calle de Las Trinitarias, you can see that an entire block is taken up by the austere brick facade of the convent.

Calle de las Huertas

Turn right up calle de las Huertas, a pedestrianised street lined with bars. Look down at the pavement, where quotes by authors including Galdós and Cervantes are set into the paving stones in brass letters.

The neoclassical building on the left on the corner with calle León was designed by Juan de Villanueva in 1788 and houses the **Real Academia de la Historia** (Royal History Academy). It was built for the monks of El Escorial (see page 82), who printed and sold their prayer books here.

On the right, on the corner of calle del Príncipe, the **Palacio de Santoña** is now the Chamber of Commerce and Industry. Built in 1734 by Pedro de Ribera, it features one of his typically elaborate Baroque doorways. Peek in the door to see the pretty courtyard.

Almost opposite is the **Casa Alberto** tavern, see ❷, with a red wooden frontage, which is a good spot for a drink, including Madrid's typical vermouth. In the early seventeenth century, Cervantes lived for a while at a house on this site.

Iglesia de San Sebastián

At the end of calle de las Huertas, a florist now stands on the site of the cemetery of the adjacent **Iglesia de San Sebastián** ❺ (free). The olive tree remains as a tribute to the many literary and theatrical figures who were buried here, including Lope de Vega, whose remains were later moved elsewhere. The church was rebuilt in the mid-twentieth century after being almost totally destroyed in the Civil War.

Calle de las Huertas opens into the Plaza del Ángel. On the left is the **Café Central**, see ❸, a leading venue for live jazz and a good place for a drink or a meal.

Take calle Espoz y Mina to the right from the square to the intersection with calle Cruz. This is where the Corral de la Cruz, one of Madrid's first theatres, was set up in the late-sixteenth century. Look up to the

Bars in the Barrio de Las Letras

Food and drink

1 Cervecería Alemana
Plaza de Santa Ana 6;
www.cerveceriaalemana.com; €
With marble tables and waiters in
white jackets, this bar has changed
little since it was founded in 1904.
It is a popular spot for breakfast, a
coffee or a beer with some tapas.
The fried fish dishes are excellent.

2 Casa Alberto
Calle Huertas 18;
www.casaalberto.es; €€
This characterful tapas bar and
restaurant has been going for
nearly two centuries. Order a
draught vermouth and try the lamb
sweetbreads and the braised oxtail.

3 Café Central
Plaza del Ángel 10;
www.cafecentralmadrid.com; €
There is live music most nights at
this characterful café with red velvet
banquettes. They serve drinks and food
all day. In the afternoon, it is a good
place to read with a cup of coffee.

4 Las Bravas
Callejón Álvarez Gato 3 (also calle Espoz
y Mina 13); https://lasbravas.com; €
You may have tried *patatas bravas*, but
the original recipe was invented in the
1930s in this no-nonsense bar. The
secret sauce is patented, but the colour
and the heat come from Spain's famous
pimentón (paprika). Share a portion
with a cold beer, and try the fried pig's
ear too if you are feeling adventurous.

right to see a large mural portraying
a confused Philip IV, searching in
vain for the theatre that was a focus
of social life during his reign – and
where he had a notorious affair
with one of the leading actresses
of the day, La Calderona.

The callejón de Álvarez Gato on
the right is named after a fifteenth-
century poet. The mirrors along
this alley commemorate the spot
where two characters in Ramón del
Valle-Inclán's play *Luces de Bohemia*
(Bohemian Lights, 1924) stand in
front of the concave, convex and

normal mirrors of an ironmonger's
that used to be situated here and
comment on the similarity between
their distorted reflections and the way
writers and artists portray society.

Las Bravas, see 4, on the left
claims to be the place where *patatas
bravas* were invented. At the end
of the alley, look at the colourful
tiled wall of Tablao Flamenco
1911, formerly named Villa Rosa
(https://tablaoflamenco1911.com/
en), a well-known flamenco club.
From the corner, turn right to arrive
back in the Plaza de Santa Ana.

The Iglesia de San Sebastián

WALK 8
The Rastro Market and Lavapiés

This walk, which explores the characterful streets sloping down from the Plaza Mayor, is more about traditions than sights. On Sunday mornings, crowds flock to the Rastro flea market, which is a real institution in the city.

DISTANCE: 3km (2 miles)
TIME: Half a day
START: Plaza de Cascorro
END: La Casa Encendida
POINTS TO NOTE: Although the market only takes place on Sundays (until 3pm), this is an interesting area to explore at any time. Beware, theft is rife on market day.

Madrid lore says Lavapiés was the medieval Jewish quarter, but the area was not part of the city until well after the Jewish population was expelled or forced to convert in 1492. Some historians think it might have been a *converso* (Jews forced to convert to Christianity) neighbourhood in the 1500s. This area is now the most multicultural in Madrid.

The Rastro

Dive into the throng at the **Plaza de Cascorro ❶** at the top of calle Ribera de Curtidores. The area buzzes with vintage shops and Sunday stalls selling bags, books and much more. Bear right along calle Amazonas to Plaza General Vara de Rey, a square filled on market day with antiques. Turn left down calle Carlos Arniches. On the left at No. 3 is the **Centro Cultural La Corrala** (free), one of Madrid's oldest surviving examples of balconied dwellings.

At the bottom of the hill is **El Capricho Extremeño**, see ❶, if you want a snack. Make your way to Plaza Campillo Mundo Nuevo, then turn left on Mira el Sol and left again back up Ribera de Curtidores.

Iglesia de San Cayetano

Turn right along calle San Cayetano to calle Embajadores and the **Iglesia de San Cayetano ❷** (www.millanycayetano.org; free). The pink brick facade dates to the late-seventeenth century but was almost totally destroyed in the Civil War and rebuilt in the 1960s.

Continue down calle Embajadores. A bit further down on the left is **Plaza Arturo Barea ❸**, renamed in 2017 in homage to the author of *The Forging of a Rebel*. On the right is the **Mercado de San Fernando**. The large brick structure

The Rastro flea market

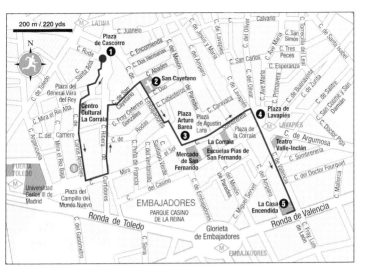

next door is the Escuelas Pías library for the Open University, built into the ruins of a church destroyed in the Civil War.

La Corrala

This pink building at the end of the square is a National Monument, and the most famous example of the galleried buildings in this district.

Plaza de Lavapiés

At the end of calle Sombrerete is **Plaza de Lavapiés ❹**, centre of the neighbourhood with several streets running north towards Sol, others east-ish towards Atocha, and anchored on the south by the **Teatro Valle-Inclán** (http://cdn.mcu.es/el-cdn/valle-inclan).

La Casa Encendida

Head down calle Valencia to ronda de Valencia, to the early twentieth-century neo-Mudéjar **La Casa Encendida ❺** (www.lacasaencendida.es; free), a dynamic cultural centre.

Food and drink

❶ El Capricho Extremeño

Calle Carlos Arniches 30;
tel: 680 347 064; €
This family-run place only opens on weekends to serve slabs of toast with tasty toppings including prawns, octopus, ham and cheese.

Plaza Corrala in Lavapiés

WALK 9
Chueca, Malasaña and Conde Duque

On this walk through the lively barrios north of the Gran Vía, full of bars, boutiques and pretty buildings with flower-filled balconies, you see how modern trends have given traditional Madrid a new lease of life.

> **DISTANCE:** 2.5km (1.5 miles)
> **TIME:** Three hours
> **START:** Plaza del Rey
> **END:** Centro Cultural Conde Duque
> **POINTS TO NOTE:** Do this walk in the early evening for the best atmosphere. It links well with walks 1 and 10 or with shopping on calle Fuencarral.

The are three distinct neighbourhoods explored on this walk: fashionable Chueca is Madrid's main LGBTQ+ area; bohemian Malasaña has smartened up and is now as popular in the day as it is at night, while elegant Conde Duque has a less frantic, more cultural vibe. Along the way, there are some interesting museums, galleries and churches, as well as lots of cafés and shops.

Plaza del Rey

Our walk starts near Plaza de Cibeles on **Plaza del Rey ❶**. The square is dominated by the Ministerio de Cultura (Ministry of Culture),

which has annexed the restored **Casa de la Siete Chimeneas**, named after its seven chimneys. One of the oldest buildings in the city, it dates back to 1577 and is rumoured to be haunted. The steel abstract sculpture is by Eduardo Chillida and the statue is of Lieutenant Jacinto Ruiz, one of the heroes of the 1808 battle against the French.

Walk up calle Barquillo and turn left on calle Augusto Figueroa. Have a look in the **Mercado de San Antón**, see ❶, a gastromarket on several floors. Or if you just fancy an ice cream, pop up the street to **Mistura**, see ❷.

Opposite the market, cut through to the **Plaza de Chueca ❷**, the heart of the neighbourhood with its many café terraces. On the north side of the square is one of Madrid's most traditional taverns, the **Taberna de Ángel Sierra**, see ❸.

Sociedad General de Autores

Walk up calle Gravina and turn right on calle Pelayo. At the end, on the corner of calle Fernando VI, is the extraordinary sight of the **Sociedad**

The Mercado de San Antón

General de Autores ❸ (Society of Authors and Editors), where strange forms of plant life seem to be oozing out of the walls. The building, designed in 1902 by Catalan architect José Grases Riera, is the best example of Art Nouveau architecture in Madrid.

Continue along calle Fernando VI, which becomes calle Mejía Lequerica. At the corner of Mejia Lequerica and Hortaleza is La Comunal, a great shop for olive oil. This corner building is the **Casa de los Lagartos** (House of the Lizards). Look up to see the stone lizards "holding up" the cornice.

Museo del Romanticismo

Take the first left along calle San Mateo, where on the right at No. 13 is the **Museo del Romanticismo** ❹ (Museum of Romanticism; www. mecd.gob.es; charge). This charming museum gives a fascinating insight into the Romantic Movement, which emerged in Spain in the 1820s. This was the house of the Marquis of Vega-Inclán (1845–1942), who was a leading exponent of the movement. Highlights include paintings by Goya and Leonardo Alenza. One room is devoted to the satirist Mariano Jose de Larra, who shot himself at the age of 28 following a doomed love affair.

Museo de la Historia de Madrid

Continue along calle San Mateo and turn right on calle Fuencarral, which is lined with boutiques. On your right is the **Museo de la Historia de Madrid** ❺ (Museum of the History of Madrid; www.madrid.es/museodehistoria; free). Originally an orphanage, the building was designed by Pedro de Ribera in the eighteenth century. The displays chart Madrid's development from medieval time to the 1900s (earlier history is dealt with at the Museo de San Isidro, see page 35). It is worth going in just to see the extraordinary wooden scale model of Madrid made in 1830 by León Gil de Palacio. As of summer 2024, the model was under restoration.

Malasaña

Opposite the museum, walk down calle San Vicente Ferrer. You are now in **Malasaña**, a neighbourhood of red-brick apartment blocks built at the turn of the twentieth century with an abundance of bars and independent shops. The area gets its name from Manuela Malasaña, a teenage seamstress who was a heroine of the uprising against Napoleon's troops, which took place nearby on May 2, 1808.

Turn right down calle San Andrés. On the left, look at the tiled walls from a former pharmacy, which were made in 1920 and show miracle cures for whooping cough and tuberculosis (building is under restoration from summer 2024, tiles not visible).

Plaza del Dos de Mayo

At the bottom of the hill is the **Plaza del Dos de Mayo** ❻. Desperate

Outside the Museo del Romanticismo

Sociedad General de Autores

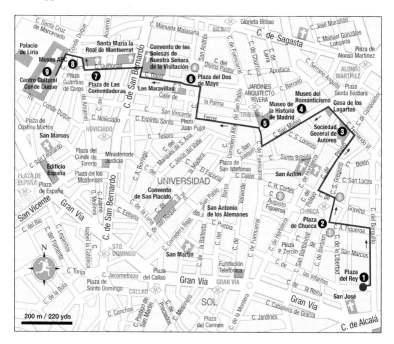

madrileños tried to arm themselves with weapons stored in an artillery barracks that stood here. The monument in the square commemorates Captains Velarde and Daoíz, who led the defence and died in the fighting. The atmosphere is much more peaceful now, with plenty of places to stop for a drink or a bite to eat, including **Cabreira**, see .

From the square, walk down Calle Daoíz to calle San Bernardo. On the right is the **Convento de las Salesas de Nuestra Señora de la Visitación,** or **Salesas Nuevas**, to differentiate from another monastery with a similar name (free) where you can buy biscuits made by the nuns at the entrance.

On the opposite side of calle San Bernardo is the **Iglesia de Santa María la Real de Montserrat** (free). Its Baroque tower was designed by Pedro de Ribera in the eighteenth century.

Plaza de las Comendadoras

Walk along calle Quiñones, by the side of the church, to the tranquil **Plaza de**

The corner of Plaza de las Comendadoras

las Comendadoras **❼** in the pleasant Conde Duque neighbourhood. Taking up the entire right side of the square is the **Convento de las Comendadoras de Santiago**. Built in the seventeenth and eighteenth centuries for the nuns protected by the knights of the Order of Santiago (St James), the convent was designed by Sabatini and the church by Manuel and José del Olmo. Temporarily closed for remodelling, with plans to create a visitor's centre for the Camino de Santiago pilgrimage.

Turn right out of the square up calle Amaniel to reach the **Museo ABC ❽** (http://museo.abc.es; free), a museum devoted to drawing, illustration and graphic design. It's housed in the first brewery for Madrid's Mahou beer; the chimney visible from Plaza Comendadoras was part of the brewery. The late nineteenth-century neo-Mudéjar building was redesigned by Spanish architects, Aranguren and Gallegos to adapt it to its new use.

Centro Cultural Conde Duque

Just above the museum, turn left into calle Montserrat, which leads to the **Centro Cultural Conde Duque ❾** (http://condeduquemadrid.es; free), set in the former barracks of the Royal Guard. Designed by Pedro de Ribera in 1717, it is now used for exhibitions as well as film, theatre and dance, and also as a library and study room, offering quiet getaways if you need to sit and relax.

Food and drink

❶ Mercado de San Antón
Calle Augusto Figueroa 24; www.mercadosananton.com; €
Chueca's neighbourhood food market has been rebuilt to suit modern tastes with gourmet stalls, tapas places and a roof terrace.

❷ Mistura
Calle Augusto Figueroa 5; http://misturaicecream.com; €
The founders of this artisan shop and café use methods learned in India to create delicious ice creams with no artificial ingredients. Good juices and coffee too.

❸ Taberna de Ángel Sierra
Calle Gravina 11; https://tabernadeangelsierra.es; €
Founded in 1917, the tavern has a tiled interior and a zinc bar. The beer and draught vermouth are excellent, accompanied by simple tapas.

❹ Cabreira
Calle Ruiz 2, Plaza Dos de Mayo; www.cabreira.es; €
You can have a beer at the bar, tapas or a full meal. Try the *patatas a la churri* – fried potatoes with scrambled egg, onion and garlic. There is another branch nearby at calle Velarde 13, which is open Mondays.

Plaza del Dos de Mayo, with the two marble statues of Velarde and Daoíz

WALK 10
From Plaza de España to the Casa de Campo

Exploring the west of Madrid takes you to a quirky museum, an Egyptian temple and a church with Goya frescoes, before walking along the newly-developed banks of the Manzanares River to the city's biggest park.

DISTANCE: 4km (2.5 miles)
TIME: Half a day
START: Plaza de España
END: Casa de Campo
POINTS TO NOTE: You could vary this walk, taking the cable car and going to the zoo and funfair, to make it more child-friendly. It combines well with the latter parts of walks 9 and 11. The cable car is closed for rebuilding until 2026.

This walk is less urban than most of the others, going mostly through parkland. In the Casa de Campo, you almost feel like you are in the countryside.

Plaza de España

The large, landscaped **Plaza de España** ❶ at the end of the Gran Vía has lots of benches, playgrounds, a bike lane and an enormous space on the north side of the square for fairs, a summer cinema and other celebrations like LGBTQ+ Pride. The landmark at the centre of the square is a monument to Cervantes, preceded by statues of Don Quixote and Sancho Panza, sculpted by Coullaut Valera in 1915.

At the top of the square is the colossal **Edificio España**, a typical example of the grand-scale architecture of Franco's dictatorship. Completed in 1953, it was the tallest building in Spain at the time. Designed by Joaquín and Julián Otamendi, over the decades the building has been occupied by offices, flats, shops and restaurants. After prolonged discussion about ownership and extensive remodelling, the Edificio España eventually opened as a *Riu* chain luxury hotel in 2019.

The Otamendi brothers were also responsible for the 32-storey **Torre de Madrid** on the north side of the square, built four years later. The *Barceló Torre de Madrid* hotel (see page 96) now occupies the first nine floors, with flats and offices above.

Just off the square is the **Palacio de Liria** (www.fundacioncasadealba. com). The eighteenth-century

Homage to Cervantes in Plaza de España

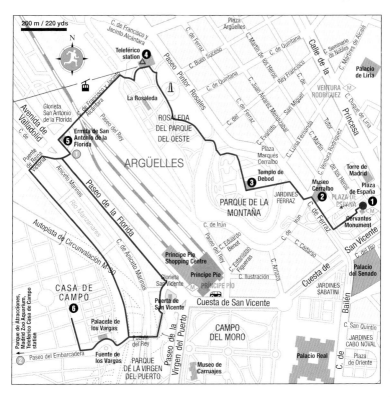

palace belongs to the House of Alba and contains an astounding art collection, but public access is strictly limited, book months in advance.

Museo Cerralbo

Walk down to the bottom of Plaza de España and turn right up calle Ferraz. On the first corner on the right is the

Museo Cerralbo 2 (www.mecd.gob.es/mcerralbo; charge). Housed in the grand residence of its founder, the Marquis of Cerralbo, this fascinating museum gives an insight into aristocratic life in Madrid in the late 1800s and early 1900s. The Marquis was an eccentric character who travelled widely, bringing all sorts of objects back from his trips.

Museo Cerralbo interior

The iconic Edificio España

Templo de Debod

Return to calle Ferraz and turn right to the traffic lights. Cross the street to reach the **Parque del Oeste** (West Park). Turn left to the stairs, at the upper level is the **Templo de Debod** ❸ (www.esmadrid.com; free). The temple was given to Spain in 1968 in thanks for the work of Spanish archeologists who had helped salvage the temples of Abu Simbel. More than 2,000 years old, it was rebuilt stone by stone, and still faces east-west, as it did originally.

Starting at the end of the reflecting pool, walk north through the park, roughly parallel to Ferraz–Paseo Pintor Rosales. When the park walkway reaches the junction of Rosales and a paved road, cross here and take a dirt path diagonally downhill to reach the upper gate of the **Rosaleda** garden, where around six hundred varieties of rose are grown. Straight ahead from the garden gate is the **Teleférico station** ❹ (www.teleferico. com; temporarily closed until 2026),

Walk down the steps by the station and continue down the path through the park, passing a small cemetery for the victims shot near here by the French on May 3, 1808.

Ermita de San Antonio de la Florida

Cross the bridge over the railway tracks to reach the **Ermita de San Antonio de la Florida** ❺ (www.esmadrid.com;

Saint Anthony's day

On June 13, the feast day of St Anthony, hundreds of women of all ages take part in one of Madrid´s more curious customs, thought to have been started by seamstresses. The saint is apparently able to rustle up lovers for anyone who might require one – or more. The hopeful participants have to drop 13 pins into the church font, which is taken outside into the garden to accommodate the crowds, then put the palm of their hand on top to see how many stick to it. The number of pins that stick indicates the number of boyfriends they can expect to come along in the year to come.

free). The dome of this neoclassical church is decorated with frescoes painted by Goya in 1798. He completed the work in only four months, which earned him the role of court painter. They depict Saint Anthony, who brings a murdered man back to life to declare the innocence of the saint's father, who had been accused of the crime.

Underneath the dome is Goya's tomb, erected in 1919 when his remains were brought from Bordeaux, where he died in 1828.

Next to the chapel is **Casa Mingo**, see ❶, an Asturian tavern and a Madrid institution.

To reach the Casa de Campo there are two options. First is walking south

Cyclists in Casa de Campo, one of the biggest parks in Europe

along calle Virgen del Puerto to a large roundabout. On the left, part of the Príncipe Pío train station is now a large shopping centre. The arch up ahead is the **Puerta de San Vicente**, a replica of the original designed in the eighteenth century by Sabatini. Turn down to the right on a pedestrian walkway and cross the river to reach the entrance to the Casa de Campo.

The second option is to cross the river at the bridge just opposite Casa Mingo, then turn left on a walkway along the river. This is the north part of **Madrid Río park,** a seven-kilometer riverside park built on top of the M-30 ring road. The construction project totally transformed the area, facilitating access to both the **Manzanares River** and the **Casa de Campo park**. Now a favourite place for walking and cycling, there are also playgrounds, rope gyms, two short zip lines and several outdoor cafés.

One of the most ambitious parts of the project was re-wilding the river itself, by first opening the seven urban dams to let the river start the process, then helping with vegetation and narrowing the channel. This was very successful, and now there is a lot of bird life along the river, from ducks to geese to egrets, cormorants and more.

Casa de Campo

The main entrance to the **Casa de Campo ❻** is marked by a semi-circle of white pillars. Now one of the biggest parks in Europe, it was created by Felipe II in the 1500s as a hunting ground near and given to the city by Alfonso XIII when he abdicated in 1931. The paved road straight ahead from the entrance leads to the boating lake, bordered by restaurants with terrace tables. One of the best spots overlooking the water is **La Parrilla del Embarcadero**, see ❷.

You can take the metro back to the city centre from Lago station, near the lake, or get the Teleférico cable car (temporarily closed for renovations until 2026) by going farther west into the park on the paved road then following signs uphill to the right to reach the opposite end of the Teleférico line.

Food and drink

❶ Casa Mingo
Paseo de la Florida 2;
www.casamingo.es; €
Open since 1888, this very popular restaurant with outdoor tables specialises in Asturian cooking with spit-roast chicken, Cabrales blue cheese and cider brewed on the premises. Takeaway available.

❷ La Parrilla del Embarcadero
Paseo del Embarcadero;
tel: 914 631 024; €€
There are lovely views of the lake at this friendly restaurant, which specialises in grilled meats.

The Templo de Debod looks its best lit up at night

WALK 11
Around Moncloa

It is worth going to the area around Madrid's main university to get off the tourist beat and visit the important Museo de América before relaxing in the delightful Parque del Oeste.

DISTANCE: 5km (3 miles)
TIME: Half a day
START: Cuartel General del Ejército del Aire y del Espacio.
END: Plaza de España
POINTS TO NOTE: You can link this with walk 10 when you get to the park, although this will involve a lot of walking if you visit all the sights along the way.

The Moncloa area spreads out around the top of calle Princesa. A key location in the Civil War, it has several examples of the mock-Habsburg architecture and monuments that were built after the conflict. Nowadays, the thousands of students who attend the sprawling university mean there is always a lively, laidback atmosphere.

Moncloa

Take the metro to Moncloa station. You emerge on calle Princesa by the immense **Cuartel General del Ejército del Aire y del Espacio ❶**, which is the headquarters of the Spanish

air force. Built in the 1940s by Luis Gutiérrez Soto, the Habsburg-style building has slate roofs and slender spires. It is so similar to the Escorial monastery that back when the building was the Air Ministry, left-wing jokers called it the Air Monastery.

This area an access point to the **Universidad Complutense**. The university was founded in Alcalá de Henares by Cardinal Cisneros in 1499 and transferred to Madrid in 1936.

Up ahead is the **Arco de la Victoria ❷**, a triumphal arch that commemorates General Franco's military victory on taking control of Madrid in the Civil War in 1939.

Faro de Moncloa

Cross Calle Princesa, passing a circular temple built as a monument to Franco's soldiers who died in the conflict, but now used by the City Council. Cross the street on your left and bear first left, then turn right onto a pedestrian walkway to reach the **Faro de Moncloa ❸** (Moncloa Lighthouse; charge). This tower has a circular observation deck with panoramic

Cuartel General del Aire, the headquarters of the Spanish air force

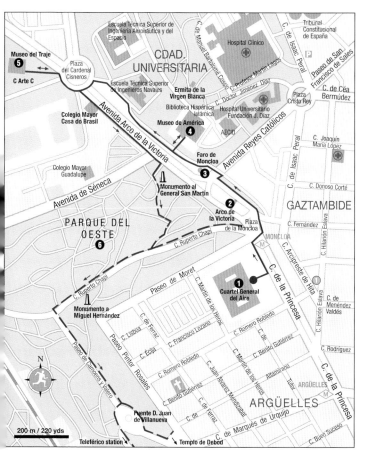

views across Madrid. Next to the
university campus, look for the Palacio
de la Moncloa, the official residence
of the Spanish prime minister.

View of Madrid from the Faro del Moncloa

Museo de América

Immediately adjacent is the **Museo
de América** ❹ (Museum of America;
www.mecd.gob.es; charge). The

large museum deals with the ancient civilisations and cultures of Spain's former colonies in Latin America, with superlative collections of art, ceramics, maps, jewellery and sacred objects.

Museo del Traje

It is a 10-minute walk up the Avenida de la Memoria (or take bus Nos. 46 or 160) to the **Museo del Traje CIPE 5** (Clothing Museum and Ethnological Heritage Research Centre; Avenida Juan de Herrera 2; www.mecd.gob.es/mtraje; free Sat after 2.30pm and Sun). The museum charts the development of what people have been wearing from the late sixteenth century to current times. Exhibits include Spanish regional costumes and clothes by leading twentieth- and twenty-first-century Spanish designers, including Balenciaga and Paco Rabanne. There is a good café as well as a book and gift shop.

Return to Moncloa. If you feel like an ice cream, head to **Los Alpes**, see 1, before going into the **Parque del Oeste 6** on the right – unless you are in the mood for shopping, in which case just walk down Calle Princesa with its boutiques and El Corte Inglés department store.

Parque del Oeste

From the corner of calle Princesa and Paseo Moret, take calle Ruperto Chapi down to **Glorieta del Maestro**. Alternatively, follow the map for this walk after visiting the Museo del Traje,

Food and drink

1 Los Alpes
Calle Arcipreste de Hita 6; www.heladeriaslosalpes.es
This family-run place opened in 1950 and serves around 50 varieties of homemade ice cream. The most popular is *mantecado*, made with egg yolk.

entering the park from Avenida de Seneca and going diagonally down. Cross the small stream, then up again to reach the Glorieta del Maestro. The lovely L-shaped park slopes from Moncloa down towards Plaza de España and the Manzanares River. It was designed at the beginning of the twentieth century by the landscape gardener Cecilio Rodríguez but had to be replanted after suffering severe damage during the Civil War; some of the older monuments bear bullet scars from that conflict. It was also the scene of fighting in the 1808 uprising against the French.

From the Glorieta (a roundabout named in honour of teachers) turn left (south) along the Paseo de Camoens, to a roundabout with a big fountain. Turn left uphill to reach the **Paseo del Pintor Rosales**, where you can sit at one of the pavement cafés before continuing towards Plaza de España. This final part of the park is covered in walk 10.

Inside the Museo de América

TOUR 12
The Paseo de la Castellana

A showcase of twentieth- and twenty-first-century architecture, the Paseo de la Castellana is the city's main north–south axis, stretching for 5km (3 miles) from the Plaza de Colón with a string of superb museums along the way.

> **DISTANCE:** 5km (3 miles)
> **TIME:** Half a day
> **START:** Plaza de Colón
> **END:** Plaza de Castilla
> **POINTS TO NOTE:** It is a good idea to use the No. 27 bus up the Paseo de la Castellana, for at least part of the route. If you visit all the museums, you will need a full day.

The Plaza de Colón marks the start of the Paseo de la Castellana. The busy boulevard was begun in the reign of Fernando VII but was not really established until the second half of the 1800s when it was extended as far as the Plaza San Juan de la Cruz. By the early 1900s, the new avenue was lined with palaces, most of which have been supplanted by sleek office buildings.

Plaza de Colón

The **Plaza de Colón** ❶ honours Christopher Columbus and the "discovery" of America. The neo-Gothic monument is now in the centre of the Paseo de la Castellana on the west side of the square, while the three abstract blocks on the east side– the **Jardines del Descubrimiento** (Discovery Gardens) – represent Columbus's ships. The **Teatro Fernán Gómez – Centro Cultural de la Villa**, a municipal theatre and cultural centre is on a lower level on the west side of the square.

East of the square is the elegant Salamanca district, devised by the flamboyant Marquis of Salamanca and built between 1860 and 1920. Now Goya, Serrano and adjoining streets are Madrid's smartest shopping area (see page 21).

The south side of the square is taken up by the **Biblioteca Nacional de España** (National Library of Spain; www.bne.es). Designed by Francisco Jareño in the second half of the nineteenth century, it has a museum and holds temporary exhibitions.

Museo Arqueológico Nacional

The rear of the library building (entrance on calle Serrano) is occupied

Puerta de Europa, rising up above busy Plaza de Castilla

by the **Museo Arqueológico Nacional** (www.man.es; charge), one of the most important museums in Spain. Allow at least two hours as there is a lot to see, including the Lady of Elche, a masterpiece of Iberian sculpture from the late fifth or early sixth century BC. Outside, you'll find a replica of the Altamira caves in Cantabria.

Opposite the Biblioteca Nacional, is the **Museo de Cera** (Wax Museum; http://museoceramadrid.com; charge), with waxworks of Picasso, Tom Cruise and Rafael Nadal. The twin towers on the northwest corner of Plaza de Colón topped by separate boxes are the **Torres Colon**, designed by Antonio Lamela in the 1970s; a major renovation finalised in 2024. Below the towers where calle Génova meets the Castellana lies the voluptuous *Woman with Mirror* sculpture by Columbian artist Fernando Botero.

Before heading up the Paseo de la Castellana, stop at **Platea Madrid**, see ❶, for some refreshment.

Paseo de la Castellana

Walking north up the central boulevard of the Paseo de la Castellana, on the right at No. 34 is the **ABC building** with its Andalusian-tiled facade, now a shopping centre.

Under the flyover nearby are some sculptures – grandly called the **Museo de Esculturas al Aire Libre** ❷ (Museum of Open-air Sculpture) – including *Stranded Mermaid* by Eduardo Chillida.

The Lady of Elche, Museo Arqueológico Nacional

Museo Sorolla

One long block further up, at the Glorieta de Emilio Castelar junction, turn left up Paseo General Martinez Campos to the charming **Museo Sorolla ❸** (www.mecd.gob.es/msorolla; charge). Joaquín Sorolla was born in Valencia in 1863 and lived in this house from 1911–23. You may well be familiar with some of his languid beach scenes. His studio is still pretty much how it was when he lived here and contains some of his best-known paintings. The lovely garden is inspired by the Alhambra in Granada and the Reales Alcazares in Seville.

Returning to the Paseo de la Castellana, cross over to the corner of calle General Oraá. If it is time for lunch, try the **BiBo** brasserie, see ❷.

Museo Lázaro Galdiano

Walk up calle General Oraá and turn left onto calle Serrano. On your right is the **Museo Lázaro Galdiano ❹** (www.flg.es; charge), which contains one of Madrid's most interesting private art collections, housed in the Italianate palatial residence of publisher and businessman José Lázaro Galdiano (1862–1947). The extensive displays range from paintings to jewellery and antiques, with works by Bosch, Gainsborough, Rembrandt, Velázquez, Zurbarán, El Greco and Goya.

Turn right out of the museum and left along calle María de Molina to get back to the Paseo de la Castellana.

Museo Nacional de Ciencias Naturales

Next up on the right is the **Museo Nacional de Ciencias Naturales ❺** (www.mncn.csic.es). Housed in a striking late nineteenth-century building, decorated with ceramics and coloured bricks, this museum brings science to life with lots of interactive exhibits.

In a small park in front of the museum is a large open white cube, in honor of Spain's 1978 Constitution. On the Paseo itself is another Botero sculpture, this one an immense hand.

Nuevos Ministerios

The next stage of the Castellana's development began in the 1930s at the next junction, **Plaza de San Juan de la Cruz**. The entire block on the left is the **Nuevos Ministerios ❻** (New Ministries), a complex of government buildings inspired by the austere style at El Escorial (see page 82). At the top end is the underground transport hub. Rising up on the left is the high-rise complex known as **AZCA**, with a huge El Corte Inglés department store. There are more shops on the adjacent calle Orense, which runs parallel to the Castellana. The tallest building is the striking white 46-storeyed **Torre Picasso** at 157 metres (515 ft), designed by Minoru Yamasaki.

Continuing up the street, the mosaic frieze facing you is the unmistakable work of Joan Miró.

TOUR 12   NUEVOS MINISTERIOS

Museo Lázaro Galdiano

Painting at the Museo Sorolla

Food and drink

1 Platea Madrid

Goya 5–7 (Plaza de Colón);
www.plateamadrid.com; €
This gastronomic hub has a wide
range of Spanish and international
cuisines. Pop in for coffee and cake at
the Mama Framboise café or pick up
fruit to take away at Gold Gourmet.

2 Bibo

Paseo de la Castellana 52;
www.grupodanigarcia.com/en/
booking/bibo-madrid; €€
Zingy design and superb food by
Dani García, who has two Michelin
stars at his restaurant in Marbella,
make this bar and brasserie an
attractive option for lunch or dinner.
The cherry gazpacho, oxtail brioche
and fried fish are particularly tasty.

Estadio Santiago Bernabéu

Cross the Paseo de la Castellana to get
to the **Estadio Santiago Bernabéu**
❼ (https://bernabeu.realmadrid.com/
es-ES).The Real Madrid football club
was founded in 1902 and this stadium
was built in the 1940s, but has since
been extended and remodelled.
The self-guided tour includes the
impressive trophy room and press area.
You can also walk down the players'
tunnel and out on to the pitch, and
look inside the Presidential Box.

Plaza de Castilla

From the stadium, jump on a No. 27
or No. 147 bus up the Castellana, to
the **Plaza de Castilla** ❽. The white
concrete sculpture is a monument to
Calvo Sotelo, a right-wing politician
assassinated in July 1936. The
obelisk in the centre of the square
is by Santiago Calatrava. The odd
circular structure on the southeast
corner was one of Madrid's first water
towers and is your landmark to find
exhibit venues used by the Fundación
Canal (www.fundacioncanal.
com), a cultural and environmental
organisation. The smaller venue on
calle Mateo Inurria is often used for
photography and the large venue on
the Castellana has done huge and
spectacular exhibits on Pompeii,
Auschwitz, and the Berlin Wall.

Dominating the junction are the
two inward-leaning towers, the **Puerta
de Europa** (Gateway to Europe),
which mark the start of Madrid's new
business area, as evidenced by the
skyscrapers rising up behind them,
still known as the **Cuatro Torres**
(Four Towers), even though there
is now a fifth tower, inaugurated in
2021. The tallest is Norman Foster's
2009 tower at 248 metres (814 ft)
with 48 storeys; originally this was
called the Torre Caja Madrid but is
now known as the Torre Foster.

To get back downtown, you
could either take the bus or
Lines 1 or 10 of the metro.

The Bernabéu, Real Madrid's home stadium

WALK 13
Toledo

Approached from Madrid, the medieval city of Toledo is a spectacular sight. High on a granite hill and almost surrounded by the Tagus River, it is packed with monuments, museums and churches. To experience Toledo as its most atmospheric, try to spend an evening there.

DISTANCE: 72km (45 miles)
TIME: A full day
START: Puerta de Bisagra
END: Mercado de San Agustín
POINTS TO NOTE: The train from Puerta de Atocha station takes 30 minutes and the bus takes 90 minutes from Plaza Elíptica station.
TOLEDO TOURISM BRACELET: Special deal to see seven Toledo monuments, some off-track or not included in this walk, though this does not include the Cathedral or the Tránsito Synagogue. Especially worthwhile if staying a couple of days. You can pay online or in person and pick up the bracelet at your first monument (https://toledomonumental.com/en). There is a tourism office in the park diagonally across from the Bisagra gate, for maps or more information.

A microcosm of Spanish history, Toledo has been a Roman fortress, a Visigothic capital and a centre of Muslim culture and learning. In the eleventh century, it was reconquered by Alfonso VI and became one of the most important cities in southern Castile, with Muslims, Jews and Christians living side by side. The court's transfer to Madrid in 1561 sparked the decline which also conserved its astonishing heritage.

This walk traces an anticlockwise loop from the **Puerta Nueva de Bisagra**, with the old Bisagra gate located further along the wall beyond the new gate ❶. Facing the Renaissance gate, you can either walk right along the Paseo de Recaredo to enter through the **Puerta de Cambrón** ❷, or take the escalators up the hill and turn right at the top.

Follow the signs to the **Monasterio de San Juan de los Reyes** ❸ (www.sanjuandelosreyes.org; charge). Founded by the Catholic Monarchs, the late-Gothic structure has a cloister with filigree carvings.

Jewish Quarter

Turning right out of the monastery, following calle Reyes Católicos, you enter the old Jewish district. On the left

View across the medieval city of Toledo and the Tagus River

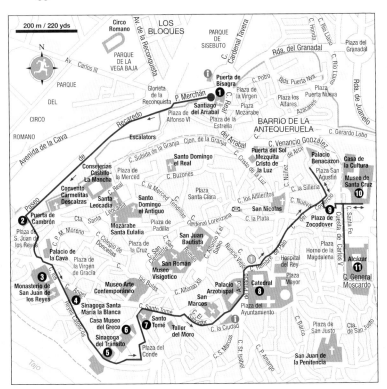

is the **Sinagoga Santa María la Blanca** ❹ (charge), a singular structure with horseshoe arches, built in the twelfth century by Muslim architects for Jews under Christian rule. At the end of the street is the **Sinagoga del Tránsito** ❺, which houses the **Museo Sefardí** (www.cultura.gob.es/msefardi; charge), charting the history of Sephardic Jews.

Founded in 1366, it is an excellent example of Mudéjar decoration.

El Greco

Adjacent is the **Casa Museo del Greco** ❻ (www.cultura.gob.es; charge), though never home to El Greco, despite the name. His masterpiece the *Burial of the Count of Orgáz* is on display in the

Toledo-steel scissors for sale

Food and drink

🟠 Adolfo

Calle Hombre de Palo 7;
www.adolforestaurante.com; €€
Adolfo Muñoz was pioneering local
produce and updating traditional
dishes in this medieval building long
before it became fashionable to do
so. Order the red partridge to savour
what Toledan cuisine is all about.

Iglesia de Santo Tomé 🟠 (https://
santotome.org; charge), nearby in
Plaza del Conde. In this work of great
spiritual intensity, the body of Gonzalo
Ruíz de Toledo is being carried by
the saints Stephen and Augustine.

Catedral

Follow the signs to the exquisite
Catedral 🟠 (www.catedralprimada.
es; charge). Begun in 1226, it was
completed in 1493. Although primarily
a superb example of Spanish Gothic,
it also has Mudéjar, Baroque and
neoclassical elements. It contains
some superb paintings by El Greco,
Titian, Van Dyck and Goya.

Plaza de Zocodover

From the cathedral, turn right up calle
Hombre de Palo, for lunch at **Adolfo**,
see 🟠. You emerge at the triangular
Plaza de Zocodover 🟠, laid out
in the late-sixteenth century on the
site of the Moorish cattle market. It
was the scene of medieval jousting
tournaments and bullfights, as well
as executions by the Inquisition.

Through the Arco de Sangre (Blood
Arch) off the square is the **Museo de
Santa Cruz 🟠** (charge), a Renaissance
orphanage and hospital housing
paintings by El Greco and Goya.

Alcázar

A few minutes' walk up the hill is the
imposing **Alcázar 🟠**, the highest point
in the city. Built in the sixteenth century,
it has a Plateresque portal by Alonso
de Covarrubias, while Juan de Herrera
designed the south facade. A Nationalist
stronghold in the Civil War, it was
relentlessly attacked by the Republicans.
Today it is home to the **Museo del
Ejército** (Army Museum; https://
ejercito.defensa.gob.es/museo; charge).

Exit through the Arco de Sangre,
heading down the hill, past several
restaurants popular with locals.

For a fun return to the bus and
train station, continue downhill
towards the river to the Alcantara
city gate. Cross the Alcantara bridge
over the Tagus and turn left to
access both train and bus stations.

If you are staying overnight, to
enhance your experience of the "City
of Three Cultures", visit El Salvador
church and Cristo de la Luz. Both
were mosques, then converted into
churches. Both are included in the
Toledo Tourism Bracelet deal.

Madonna and Child

The Cathedral's Spanish Gothic facade

WALK 14
El Escorial and Valle de los Caídos

Built by Felipe II in the sixteenth century, El Escorial makes a powerful statement about the power of the Habsburg dynasty. The vast granite structure contains a wealth of artworks, including paintings by El Greco, Titian and Rubens.

DISTANCE: 54km (33 miles)
TIME: A full day
START/END: El Escorial
POINTS TO NOTE: Take bus 661 or 664 from the Intercambiador de Moncloa, or the C3 train from Atocha, Sol, Nuevos Ministerios or Chamartín stations (both take about an hour). For the Valle de los Caídos, on weekends and October to March the 660 bus leaves San Lorenzo de El Escorial at 3.15pm; April to September at 4pm and returns at 5.30pm, on weekends and October to March, April to September at 6pm.

Allow a whole morning to visit the monastery and see the pleasant town of San Lorenzo de El Escorial. You could then have lunch before catching the bus to the Valle de los Caídos.

Real Monasterio de San Lorenzo de El Escorial

The **Real Monasterio de San Lorenzo de El Escorial** ❶ (Royal Monastery of San Lorenzo de El Escorial; www.patrimonionacional.es; charge) is a solemn structure that reflects Felipe II's austere nature and the strength of his religious devotion. It is said that the king decided that this was the perfect site on August 10, 1577, which is Saint Lawrence's day and also the date of Spain's victory over France at St Quentin. To commemorate this, the monastery is named after the saint and the parallelogram plan is said to represent the gridiron on which he was burnt to death.

The building has more than 2,600 windows and 1,200 doors. Although most of the original art collection is in the Prado Museum, there are many masterpieces on display, including works by Veronese, Tintoretto, El Greco, Ribera, Rubens, Martin de Vos and Michiel van Coxcie.

In the king's spartan chamber, the bed was positioned so that he could see the high altar of the church and also the surrounding countryside. Also part of the complex is the office from which he boasted he

The austere lines of El Escorial

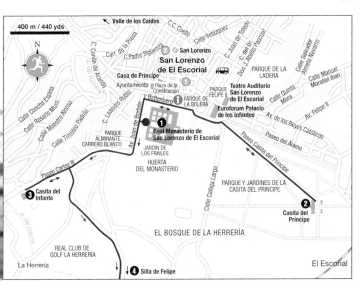

ruled the world from two inches of paper and the octagonal marble **Panteón de los Reyes**, containing the remains of nearly all the Spanish monarchs from Felipe II onwards.

The magnificent **Basílica** is crowned by a dome with a diameter of 92 metres (302 ft) set on a drum with frescoes by Luca Giordano. The **Capilla Mayor** is the spiritual powerhouse of the monastery and features a marble and gilded bronze altarpiece flanked on either side by sculptural groups by Leone Leoni of Carlos V with his family and Felipe II with three of his wives. The barrel-vaulted library, the **Biblioteca Real**,

is 55 metres (180 ft) long with a marble floor and ceiling frescoes by Tibaldi. The shelves contain more than 40,000 documents and books, arranged with the leaves facing outwards to aid conservation by allowing air to permeate the paper.

During the reign of Carlos III in the eighteenth century, Juan de Villanueva designed two lodges near the monastery for recreational purposes. The **Casita del Príncipe** ② (also known as the Casa de Abajo) is situated in the Jardínes del Príncipe down the hill to the east. The **Casita del Infante** ③ (or Casita de Arriba), about 2km (1.2 miles) along the Paseo de Carlos III, is a hunting

The exquisite Biblioteca Real at El Escorial

Food and drink

1 La Cueva
Calle San Antón 4;
www.mesonlacueva.com; €€
In a building dating back to the eighteenth century, La Cueva serves traditional Castilian dishes with tasty stews and meat roasted in a charcoal oven.

2 Montia
Calle Calvario 4; www.montia.es; €€€
Five minutes' walk from the monastery, Montia serves contemporary cuisine with a constantly changing menu of dishes created from the best local produce available. Book ahead.

pavilion that was home to Juan Carlos I, the former king, when he was a student. About 5km (3 miles) away, in the hills to the south, is the **Silla de Felipe 4** (Philip's Seat), where the king used to sit in a chair carved out of the rocks to watch his dream being realised.

Ever since the railway was built in the 1800s, *madrileños* have flocked to **San Lorenzo de El Escorial** at weekends to enjoy the cooler temperatures, and the lively cultural events and festivals throughout the summer. The town has an elegant eighteenth-century theatre, the **Coliseo Real** and some attractive bars and restaurants, including the traditional **La Cueva**, see 1 and the more creative **Montia**, see 2.

Valle de los Caídos

The **Valle de los Caídos** (Valley of the Fallen; https://valledeloscaidos.es) is the site of a basilica and monastery, marked by a cross that is visible from a great distance. Made of local granite, it is nearly 150 metres high (492 ft) with a span of 46 metres (151 ft).

Construction of the monument begun in the 1940s on the orders of General Franco, supposedly to commemorate those who died in Spain's Civil War (1936–39). After the war ended, Republican prisoners, many of whom died in the process, were drafted in to dig the site out of the rocky mountainside. Completed nearly two decades later in 1958, the basilica contains an enormous crypt that housed the tombs of General Franco and José Antonio Primo de Rivera, the founder of the far-right Falangist party. More than 30,000 soldiers, both Nationalist and Republican, are believed to be buried in the walls of the basilica and in the hillside around it.

After years of negotiations, in 2019 Franco's remains were taken to Mingorrubio where his wife was buried, and Spanish dictator Primo de Rivera was removed in 2023. Discussions continue about the future of this site, hopefully it will be a museum with a more balanced view of the monument itself and of the Civil War.

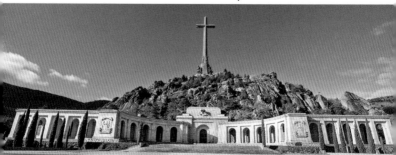
Valle de los Caídos marks the site of a basilica and monastery

WALK 15
Segovia

Set on a ridge in the Castilian countryside, Segovia is a delightful town of honey-coloured buildings and Romanesque churches, where the rich heritage mixes with a lively contemporary cultural scene. Spend the morning sightseeing before a lunch of suckling pig or roast lamb.

DISTANCE: 88km (55 miles)
TIME: A full day
START: Acueducto
END: Alcázar
POINTS TO NOTE: The train to Segovia from Chamartín station takes 30 minutes. La Sepúlvedana runs a frequent bus service from the Intercambiador de Moncloa, which takes an hour. The train station is just outside the city, requiring a short bus ride to the centre; the bus station is about a ten-minute walk from the acueducto. It is usually cooler in Segovia than Madrid, so take an extra layer.

Long before Madrid became the capital in the sixteenth century, Segovia was one of the most important cities in Spain, as borne out by the many Romanesque churches that you come across almost at every turn. The promontory, shaped like a teardrop, is a dense mesh of ochre buildings with spindly spires seeming to jostle for prime spots on the skyline.

While the old town has UNESCO World Heritage status, there is nothing staid about Segovia. Lots of palaces, churches and monasteries are now used for exhibitions and concerts. There are characterful shops too, and many come here at weekends just for a roast lunch at one of the traditional restaurants.

Acueducto

Segovia's best-known landmark, the **Acueducto ❶**, was built 2,000 years ago by the Romans and carried the city's water supply until half a century ago. Great slabs of granite from the Guadarrama mountains form 118 arches that stretch across the Plaza del Azoguejo and beyond for 813 metres/yds. It is astonishing to think that there is no cement holding the structure together.

The aqueduct stands in the **Plaza del Azoguejo**, where there is a tourist information centre. Also here is the **Mesón de Cándido**, see ❶, Segovia's most famous restaurant. From the square, calle Cervantes leads up the hill through the centre of the town. On the right is the **Casa de**

Segovia's skyline

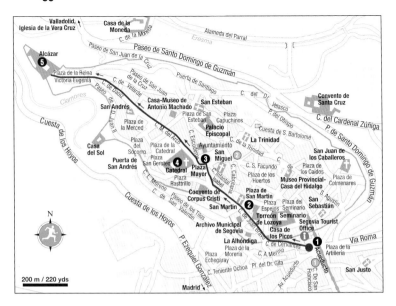

los Picos, with a sixteenth-century facade of pointed granite stones.

The street changes its name to calle Juan Bravo, who was the leader of the uprising in the 1500s when local inhabitants rebelled against Carlos V and the nobility. There is a statue of him in the **Plaza de San Martín ❷**, where the twelfth-century **Iglesia de San Martín** has a Mudéjar tower. At the top of the steps on the right is the fifteenth-century **Torreón de Lozoya**.

Plaza Mayor

Continuing up the street, you emerge in the splendid, porticoed **Plaza Mayor ❸**, with the seventeenth-century town hall facing you and several attractive cafés and restaurants. The **Mesón José María**, see ❷, one of the best traditional places to eat, is just off the square.

Catedral

On the left of the square is the **Catedral ❹** (https://catedralsegovia.es). One of the last Gothic cathedrals in Spain, this is Segovia's second cathedral, the Romanesque cathedral located next to the Alcázar was destroyed in the sixteenth-century uprising. Designed by Juan Gil de Hontañón and his son Rodrigo, the dainty

Some of the Acueducto's 118 arches

Suits of armour in the Alcázar

Food and drink

❶ Mesón de Cándido
Plaza del Azoguejo 5;
www.mesondecandido.es; €€
With a history going back more than
a century, Cándido is deservedly
renowned throughout Spain and
beyond for its roast suckling pig
and lamb, as well as other regional
specialities. Right by the aqueduct in
an historic building, eating here is the
quintessential Segovia experience.

❷ Mesón José María
Calle Cronista Lecea 11;
www.restaurantejosemaria.com; €€
Just off the Plaza Mayor, José
María serves superb roasts and
more elaborate dishes too. If you
don't want a full meal, call in for a
glass of wine in the lively bar at the
front of the restaurant, where you
get a free tapa with every drink.

structure with filigree spires was built
in the sixteenth century. The elegant
interior, softened by golden sandstone,
features stained-glass windows made
by Flemish and Spanish craftsmen.

Alcázar

Continuing past the cathedral, you reach
the **Alcázar** ❺ (www.alcazardesegovia.
com; charge). The fairy-tale castle with
slate turrets, which looks more Bavarian
than Castilian, stands at the end of
the limestone ridge at the point where
the Eresma and Clamores rivers meet.
Although there had been a fortress here
since the 1200s, this structure was built
in the second half of the 1800s after a
fire. Weapons and suits of armour are
on display in the museum and there are
panoramic views of the town and the
surrounding countryside from the tower.

The multi-sided church down in
the valley is the **Vera Cruz church**,
which was founded by the Knights of
the Holy Sepulchre in 1208 and now
belongs to the Knights of Malta. The
village on the hill is **Zamarramala**,
where the local women take over
all business and administration for
one day in February (Las Alcaldesas
fiesta), in memory of their help
conquering the Alcázar in 1227.

The hills around Segovia   The dainty Catedral

DIRECTORY

Our edit of the best hotels, restaurants and evening entertainment to suit all tastes and budgets, plus an A–Z of all the essential information you need to know, a quick language guide, and some great book and film recommendations to give you a flavour of Madrid.

Accommodation

Madrid has an excellent range of accommodation, whether you are looking for a luxury hotel or a no-frills base. Many hotels, even when part of major chains, occupy elegant late nineteenth-century buildings, with several in former palaces.

There has been a boom in recent years of stylish, inexpensive places, which usually offer pared-back rooms with good beds and showers, while not bothering with facilities that many people on a city break simply do not need.

At the top end of the market, meanwhile, there are some stunning new properties with cutting-edge design, Michelin-starred restaurants, sumptuous spas and spectacular rooftop bars.

There has been a huge growth in the holiday apartment market in the last decade – a great option for those travelling with children.

As the centre of Madrid is quite compact, you can usually walk from your hotel to most places you are likely to want to go in less than 20 minutes. Plaza de Santa Ana, Chueca and Plaza de España are good areas to base yourself. Some of the smartest hotels are in the Salamanca district, near good shops and with plenty of restaurants nearby. You might need to take a short metro or taxi ride to get to some of the museums and other sights, but there is a less touristy atmosphere than around the Puerta del Sol.

There are often bargains to be had in August, when many locals go on holiday, particularly at high-end hotels. January and February are the cheapest months.

Price categories

Price guide for a double room for one night without breakfast:
€€€€ = more than 250 euros
€€€ = 150–250 euros
€€ = 80–150 euros
€ = less than 80 euros

Puerta del Sol and the Gran Vía

Círculo Gran Vía Autograph Collection
Gran Vía 24; https://autograph-hotels.marriott.com/hotel/hotel-circulo-gran-via; €€€€
This adults-only luxury hotel occupies an ornate 1920s building on the Gran Vía. The 71 rooms in mid-century modern style are spacious and stylish and there is a gym and a roof terrace.

Dear Hotel
Gran Vía 80; www.dearhotelmadrid.com; €€
It is all about the views at the four-star *Dear Hotel*, where there are a lot of luxe touches in the 162 Scandi-

View across Madrid from the Principal

style rooms. The best vistas are from the rooftop bar and restaurant, where there is also a plunge pool.

Emperador
Gran Vía 53; www.emperadorhotel.com; €€€
The rooftop pool at the four-star *Emperador* is a haven on hot summer days. The hotel, opened in 1947, exudes traditional glamour with 232 classically designed rooms. Some have terraces and there are spectacular views from the upper floors.

Indigo
Calle Silva 6; www.indigomadrid.com; €€
The four-star *Indigo* has 85 rooms in opulent jewel shades with luxurious beds. With a bar and a pool up on the roof, it is a cool place to hang out in summer.

NH Suecia
Calle Marqués de Casa Riera 4; www.nh-collection.com/hotel/nh-collection-madrid-suecia; €€€
A favourite of Ernest Hemingway and Che Guevara, with 123 rooms and suites on ten floors. Revamped in 2016 by star designer Lázaro Rosa-Violán. Guests sip cocktails in the decadent Hemingway bar or up on the roof terrace.

Praktik Metropol
Calle Montera 47; https://praktik-metropol-hotel-madrid.at-hotels.com/es; €
This industrial-style hotel has a welcoming atmosphere with a pleasant lounge and basic but comfortable, monochrome rooms.

Principal
Calle Marqués de Valdeiglesias 1, corner Gran Vía 2; www.theprincipalmadridhotel.com; €€€
This five-star hotel set in a grand early-twentieth-century building has 76 rooms and a calming grey colour scheme. The restaurant is overseen by Michelin-starred chef Ramon Freixa and there are two chic roof terraces for cocktails and sunbathing.

Vincci 66
Gran Vía 66; www.vinccihoteles.com/eng/Hotels/Spain/Madrid/Vincci-Via-66; €€
This 1940s building has stunning features, such as a marble staircase and stained-glass windows. The 116 rooms are decorated with luxurious fabrics in crimson and gold and there are fabulous views form the tenth-floor roof terrace.

Vincci The Mint
Gran Vía 10; http://en.vinccithemint.com; €€€
With zingy design in shades of green, the four-star, fashionable hotel occupies an elegant, early twentieth-century building and has a rooftop bar with spectacular views. The 88 rooms and suites, some with terraces, are spacious and light.

Plaza Mayor and Madrid de Los Austrias
Mayerling
Calle del Conde de Romanones 6; www.mayerlinghotel.com; €€
This two-star has 22 rooms in a former fabric warehouse in a handy location.

A luxury room at the Principal

With contemporary design and a sun terrace, it is a pleasant no-frills option.

Petit Palace Posada del Peine
Calle Postas 17;
www.petitpalaceposadadelpeine.com; €€
In a characterful historic building alongside the Plaza Mayor, this four-star hotel is good for families as some of the contemporary rooms have bunks as well as double beds.

La Posada del Dragón
Calle Cava Baja 14;
www.posadadeldragon.com; €€
In the oldest and most atmospheric part of Madrid on a street lined with tapas bars, this chic three-star hotel with 27 rooms blends contemporary style with traditional architecture.

Posada del León de Oro
Calle Cava Baja 12;
www.posadadelleondeoro.com; €€
Once a coaching inn set around a courtyard, this is now a characterful four-star boutique hotel with seventeen romantic rooms. Good restaurant and a popular wine bar.

The Hat
Calle Imperial 9; www.thehatmadrid.com; €
This is a hostel with the style of a boutique hotel. Fuelled by biomass energy, with distressed wood and leather furniture in the lobby bar and a groovy roof terrace, it has double and family rooms as well as dorms.

Royal Madrid
Central Palace Madrid
Plaza de Oriente 2;
www.centralpalacemadrid.com; €€
Although lacking facilities, this quirky place has quite possibly the best location in the city, opposite the Palacio Real. On the upper floors of an elegant building, it has attractive rooms in natural tones.

Gala
Costanilla de los Angeles 15;
www.hostalgala.com; €
On the second floor (with a lift) of a nineteenth-century building within easy walking distance of shops and sights, the no-frills Gala has 22 rooms, some suitable for families, with a modern design.

Gran Meliá Palacio de los Duques
Cuesta de Santo Domingo 5;
www.melia.com/es/hoteles/espana/madrid/palacio-de-los-duques-gran-melia; €€€€
This five-star hotel with 180 rooms and suites in a lavishly remodelled palace near the Teatro Real is among the best in Madrid with superb service, outstanding food and a rooftop pool. Inside there is a Velázquez theme, inspired by the tones of his palette.

Room Mate Laura
Travesía de Trujillo 3; https://room-matehotels.com/en/laura; €€
This chic three-star hotel is hidden away from the crowds by the Descalzas Reales convent. Designer

A vast suite at Gran Meliá Palacio de los Duques

Tomás Alia has put large prints of Juana de Austria, the founder of the convent, in prime position in the loft-style rooms, some of which have kitchens and are great for families.

Room Mate Mario
Calle Campomanes 4; https://room-matehotels.com/en/mario; €€

On a quiet street near the Teatro Real and the Royal Palace, this is a smart yet inexpensive option that appeals to design fans with splashes of colour zinging up the white décor in the 54 rooms.

Room007 Select Sol
Calle de las Fuentes 13; https://roomselecthotels.com/madrid; €

With good beds and crisp contemporary design, this is a basic but attractive place to stay in a central location.

Toc
Plaza Celenque 3-5; www.tochostels.com/madrid; €€

If you want to stay somewhere comfortable, fun and reasonably priced in the centre of Madrid, this stylish hostel in a handsome building fits the bill. There are double and family rooms as well as dorms, and facilities include a kitchen.

The Paseo del Prado and the Retiro Park

Doubletree by Hilton Madrid Prado
Calle San Agustín 3; www.hilton.com/es/hotels/madprdi-doubletree-madrid-prado; €€€€

This four-star has a five-star boutique feel and is a favourite of art and fashion folk. Close to the Prado and tapas bars, it has 61 rooms in grey and indigo tones. The *Kirei* Japanese restaurant is excellent.

Only You Atocha
Paseo de la Infanta Isabel 13; www.onlyyouhotels.com/en/hotels/only-you-hotel-atocha; €€€

With a big wow factor owing to the dazzling loft-style design by Lázaro Rosa-Violán, this four-star hotel between the Retiro Park and Atocha train station has 205 rooms and suites on seven floors with lots of natural light.

Palacio del Retiro Autograph Collection
Calle Alfonso XII 14; https://autograph-hotels.marriott.com/hotel/hotel-palacio-del-retiro; €€€€

Original features contrast with contemporary design in this early twentieth-century palace, now a five-star luxury hotel. The fifty rooms and suites all have a view of the Retiro Park opposite. A grand staircase and stained-glass windows add to the grandeur.

Petit Palace Savoy Alfonso XII
Calle Alfonso XII 18; www.petitpalacesavoyalfonsoxii.com/es; €€

Shades of mauve and grey create a soothing vibe in this dainty nineteenth-century palace, situated on one of the smartest corners in the city. Bikes available.

The loft-style lobby at Only You Atocha

Ritz Madrid
Plaza de la Lealtad 5; www.mandarinoriental.
com/es-es/madrid/hotel-ritz; €€€€
Classic luxury and exquisite service
make the *Ritz* one of Madrid's top
hotels. Some rooms have chandeliers
and silk canopies over the beds and
most are furnished with antiques.
The terrace is a delightful spot
for drinks or brunch, even if you
are not staying in the hotel.

Sleep'n Atocha
Calle Dr. Drumen 4; www.sleepnatocha.com; €€
Opposite both the Reina Sofía
museum and Atocha station, this
unfussy stylish hotel has comfortable
rooms, some with balconies.

Villa Real
Plaza de las Cortes 10;
www.hotelvillareal.com; €€€
Close to the major museums, the
five-star *Villa Real* is a classic hotel
that is filled with extraordinary
artworks – antiquities include Syrian
mosaics and Greek vases. There are
115 rooms and suites, some duplex
and most with small balconies.

Wellington
Calle Velázquez 8; www.hotel-
wellington.com; €€€
The five-star *Wellington* is one of
Madrid's most renowned hotels, with
a pool and garden on the rooftop,
a luxury spa and sumptuous rooms
with marble bathrooms. The *Kabuki*

restaurant has a Michelin star and the
Goizeko offers superb Basque cuisine.

Westin Palace
Plaza de las Cortes 7; www.marriott.
com/es/hotels/madwi-the-westin-
palace-madrid/overview; €€€€
Wallow in five-star glamour at one
of Madrid's most renowned historic
hotels. The 467 spacious rooms have
deep carpets and sumptuous beds.

Plaza de Santa Ana,
the Barrio de las Letras
and Lavapiés

Artrip
Calle Valencia 11; www.artriphotel.com; €€
In multicultural Lavapiés, near the
Reina Sofía museum and Atocha train
station, this is a seventeen-room, friendly,
no-frills hotel with contemporary
design in a traditional building.

Casual Madrid del Teatro
Calle Echegaray 1; www.casualhoteles.com/
en/hotels-madrid/casual-del-teatro; €
The 37 rooms at this fun, no-frills
option are themed to recreate the sets of
musicals and plays. In a handy location,
it offers good facilities for families.

Me Madrid Reina Victoria
Plaza de Santa Ana, 14; www.melia.
com/es/hoteles/espana/madrid/
me-madrid-reina-victoria; €€€
This four-star, buzzy hotel in an
historic building in an excellent
location is really fun place to stay

Traditional room décor at the Ritz

with a great restaurant and rooftop bar. The 192 rooms and suites have purple fridges and hangover kits.

NH Collection Palacio de Tepa
Calle San Sebastián 2; www.nh-collection.com/hotel/nh-collection-madrid-palacio-de-tepa; €€€

This elegant five-star hotel occupies a palatial neoclassical building designed by Juan de Villanueva, the architect of the Prado Museum. Some rooms have vaulted or sloping wooden ceilings and there are duplex spaces that are good for families.

OK Hostel
Calle Juanelo 24; www.okhostels.com; €

Smart design, a warm vibe and a location in a less touristy, more traditional part of the centre combine to make this hostel one of the best in the city. Double rooms and dorms available.

Pasaje
Calle del Pozo 4; www.elpasajehs.com; €€

In a characterful building on a pedestrianised lane, the three-star *Pasaje* has fourteen rooms which are a bit basic but have all the facilities are you likely to need on a short stay.

Room Mate Alicia
Calle del Prado 2; https://room-matehotels.com/en/alicia; €€

Top interior designer Pascua Ortega transformed a twentieth-century industrial building into a light-filled space, which is now a favourite with fashion and media types. Pale wood contrasts with bold splashes of colour in the 34 rooms. Two splendid duplex suites have roof terraces and plunge pools.

Urban
Carretera de San Jerónimo 34; www.hotelurban.com; €€€€

This five-star is a fashionable design hotel filled with ancient Egyptian, African and Asian artefacts and contemporary artworks. A rooftop pool and the *Cebo* restaurant, one of the best in Madrid, add to the allure.

Vincci Soho
Calle del Prado 18; http://en.vinccisoho.com; €€€

Purple, pink and red tones perk up the interiors of the five nineteenth-century buildings occupied by this four-star hotel in the heart of the Barrio de Las Letras. Lavish room décor and relaxing courtyard.

Chueca, Malasaña and Conde Duque
B&B Fuencarral 52
Calle Fuencarral 52; www.hotel-bb.es/en/hotel/madrid-fuencarral-52; €€

This restored traditional building is a handy place to stay if you are planning on spending time in the fashionable Chueca and Malasaña areas. Rooms are fresh, bright and modern and there is a roof terrace with a vertical garden.

Urban's inviting rooftop pool

Eurostars Central

Mejía Lequerica 10; www.eurostarshotels.
com/eurostars-central.html; €€

Contemporary, minimalist design, combined with large rooms and a trendy rather than touristy location make this four-star hotel a good choice. The 135 rooms and suites all face outwards and those on the top floor have terraces.

Only You Boutique

Calle Barquillo 21; www.onlyyouhotels.com/en/
hotels/only-you-boutique-hotel-madrid; €€€€

The street-level bar and restaurant are popular places to meet at this chic boutique hotel in a former palatial residence remodelled by designer Lázaro Rosa-Violán. Rooms have a navy and white colour scheme and the best have spectacular terraces and are more like apartments.

Room Mate Óscar

Plaza Pedro Zerolo 12; https://room-
matehotels.com/es/oscar; €€

This is a fashionable and comfortable place to stay, located in the heart of Chueca with 74 rooms in an attractive Bauhaus-style building with peppy design by Tomás Alia, a rooftop pool and a lively vibe.

Urso

Calle Mejía Lequerica 8; www.hotelurso.com; €€€

This discreet, five-star boutique hotel is opposite the Barceló market. The palatial building retains many original features, including stained-glass windows. There is an excellent restaurant and a spa with a small pool.

Plaza de España and Moncloa

Barceló Torre de Madrid

Plaza de España 18; www.barcelo.com/
es-es/barcelo-torre-de-madrid €€€€

Top Spanish designer Jaime Hayón has created fresh interiors in jewel and berry shades at this five-star hotel with 258 rooms in the Torre de Madrid skyscraper. It has a great cocktail bar, a spa and an indoor pool.

Casón del Tormes

Calle del Río 7;
www.casondeltormes.com/es; €€

The three-star *Casón del Tormes* has a family feel and a handy location. The 63 rooms are decorated in classic style and rates are usually reasonable for the standard.

Exe Moncloa

Calle Arcipreste de Hita 10;
www.eurostarshotels.com/exe-moncloa.html; €€

There is a lively vibe at this four-star hotel in buzzy Moncloa. With a cool roof terrace, easy access to public transport and affordable rates, it is an attractive option in a less touristy area.

Meliá Madrid Princesa

Calle Princesa 27; www.melia.com/es/hoteles/
espana/madrid/melia-madrid-princesa ; €€€

This well-established five-star hotel has 269 comfortable, modern

Clean lines at Urso

rooms, superb service, and it sits in a convenient location. It's a popular option with frequent travellers who need a hotel with guaranteed standards throughout.

Paseo de la Castellana and Salamanca

AC Recoletos
Calle Recoletos 18; www.marriott.com/hotels/travel/madrc-ac-hotel-recoletos; €€€
The four-star *Paseo de la Castellana and Salamanca*, originally a grand private residence, combines neoclassical style with minimalist chic interiors. On a quiet street near the shops on calle Serrano, the Retiro Park, the Plaza de Cibeles and the airport bus stop, it is a convenient, comfortable base.

Barceló Emperatriz
Calle López de Hoyos 4; www.barceloemperatriz.com; €€€€
This ultra-stylish five-star hotel is inspired by Eugenia de Montijo, the nineteenth-century Empress who was married to Napoleon III. It feels grand and palatial but in a contemporary rather than a stuffy way. The 146 rooms have beautiful bathrooms and there is a small pool on the roof terrace. Ideal if you're looking for some quiet luxury.

Hyatt Regency Hesperia Madrid
Paseo de la Castellana 57; www.hesperia-madrid.com; €€€
This five-star hotel was revamped by Pascua Ortega, one of Spain's most well-known interior designers. The 171 rooms and suites combine traditional style with Art Deco features and contemporary touches. It also features the *Santceloni* restaurant, which boasts two Michelin stars.

NH Collection Colón
Calle Marqués de Zurgena 4; www.nh-collection.com/es/hotel/nh-collection-madrid-colon; €€€
Designed in the mid-twentieth century by renowned architect Luis Gutiérrez-Soto, the four-star hotel was totally remodelled in 2016. It has 146 rooms and suites, an outdoor pool and a good gym. It's also in a handy location if you're interested in visiting Madrid's best shopping streets.

Tótem
Calle Hermosilla 23; www.totem-madrid.com; €€€
Occupying one of the most prestigious corners in the city, the four-star *Tótem* has 67 rooms in contemporary style in tones of grey and blue. It feels a bit like a private club, and features a stylish bar and restaurant.

Único
Calle Claudio Coello 67; www.unicohotelmadrid.com; €€€€
This five-star hotel has 44 rooms and suites and occupies an elegant nineteenth-century palace on one of Madrid's most exclusive streets. It feels rather peaceful and luxurious, and its *Ramon Freixa* restaurant has two Michelin stars.

Contemporary style at Tótem

Restaurants

The streets of Madrid are packed with places to eat and drink, ranging from basic bars to elegant Michelin-starred restaurants. Walking around the city, you come across stylish cafés, boisterous tapas bars, chic gastrobars, classic Castilian restaurants and more informal brasseries with contemporary design.

Lots of locals eat out every day and most *madrileños* pop into their neighbourhood bar for a coffee, a beer, a snack and a chat at some point in the day.

The usual restaurant opening hours are 1pm to 4pm for lunch and 9pm until midnight for dinner, although these times are becoming increasingly flexible. *Madrileños* tend to arrive at a restaurant between 2pm and 3pm for lunch, while 10pm is the key booking time for dinner, so it is much easier to get a table without a reservation if you pitch up an hour earlier than those key times. For anywhere except very high end or fashionable restaurants, you do not usually have to book more than a day or two in advance. Friday and Saturday nights are by far the busiest, while on Sunday evenings and all-day Monday or Tuesday places are most likely to be closed. A lot of restaurants shut for at least two weeks in August.

Tapas bars keep similar hours for lunch, but get going earlier

in the evening, from around 8pm. Cafés are open all day.

> ### Price categories
> Price guide based on a two-course meal with one glass of wine:
> €€€€ = more than 60 euros
> €€€ = 40–60 euros
> €€ = 25–40 euros
> € = less than 25 euros

Puerta del Sol and the Gran Vía

La Casa del Abuelo
Calle Victoria 12; www.lacasadelabuelo.es; €
This frantically busy family-run bar is an essential stop for a vermouth or a beer with a dish of prawns sizzling away in olive oil pepped up with garlic and chili.

Lhardy
Carrera de San Jerónimo 8; https://lhardy.com; €€€
You may well spot a politician, actor or writer at *Lhardy*, which opened in 1839. You can have a drink in the shop, where ornate cabinets display dainty sandwiches, or eat in one of the grand dining rooms. Their *cocido* stew is renowned.

La Tasquita de Enfrente
Calle Ballesta 6; www.latasquitadeenfrente.com; €€€€

The family-run La Casa del Abuelo tapas bar

Book ahead at Juanjo López Bedmar's tiny restaurant in the Triball area, which is one of the best in town and a favourite of foodies and off-duty chefs. The ultra seasonal tasting menu features the best of Spanish produce.

La Terraza del Casino
Calle Alcalá 15;
www.pacoroncerorestaurante.com/en; €€€€
Paco Roncero's flagship restaurant has two Michelin stars and occupies an impressive space at the top of the Casino de Madrid private club. Expect to be surprised by every dish. With a romantic terrace, this is a spot for a special occasion.

Plaza Mayor and Madrid de Los Austrias
Botín
Calle Cuchilleros 17; www.botin.es; €€€
Founded in 1725, *Botín* is officially the oldest restaurant in the world and was a favourite of Ernest Hemingway. The roast suckling pig or lamb are the dishes to devour in one of the tiled dining rooms or in the vaulted cellar.

Casa Revuelta
Calle Latoneros 3; www.casarevuelta.com/en; €
Founded in the 1960s, *Casa Revuelta* is one of the most traditional taverns in Madrid. People come here just for the tortilla potato omelette, but the cod strips in batter and the meatballs in tomato sauce are legendary too.

Los Galayos
Calle Botoneras 5; www.losgalayos.net; €€
With a terrace on the Plaza Mayor and a brick-vaulted dining room, *Los Galayos* is as traditional as it gets. Open since 1894, come here for local dishes such as suckling pig and *cocido* stew. Or just have tapas at the seventeenth-century wooden bar.

La Musa
Costanilla de San Andrés 12, Plaza de la Paja; https://grupolamusa.com/restaurante-musa-latina; €
With tables in the square and a buzzy vibe inside, *La Musa* is always busy. The menu has something to suit everyone, with a mix of Mediterranean and Asian dishes to share.

Taberna Los Huevos de Lucio
Calle Cava Baja 30;
https://loshuevosdelucio.com/taberna; €€
Run by the younger generation of the family behind revered restaurant *Casa Lucio* across the street, the signature dish at this more informal tavern is *huevos rotos* – fried eggs broken over a pile of chips with ham or *pisto* (similar to ratatouille). Sit at the bar or book a table in the attractive dining room at the back.

Royal Madrid
El Anciano Rey de los Vinos
Calle Bailén 19;
www.elancianoreydelosvinos.es; €
This traditional tavern with outdoor tables has been open for more than

Dining at Los Galayos on Plaza Mayor

Opera Victoria

a century. Opposite the Almudena cathedral and close to the Royal Palace, it is a handy spot for a drink – try their own-label wine or draught vermouth – or a sit-down meal.

De María
Plaza de Isabel II 8;
www.demariarestaurante.es; €€
Specialises in Argentinian grilled meat dishes. As well as excellent steaks, the menu includes pasta and salads. Friendly staff. Several branches around the city.

Opera Victoria
Calle Caños de Peral 2 (northeast corner Opera square); https://andilana.com/locales/opera-victoria; €€

Inside Botín, the oldest restaurant in the world

Opera Victoria has a good international style menu and good fixed-price meals, especially Monday to Friday at lunch. The décor is nice and there is an outdoor area. Part of a hotel-restaurante group from Catalonia, there are several other restaurants in Madrid.

El Pato Mudo
Costanilla de los Ángeles 8;
https://elpatomudomadrid.com; €€
This small restaurant specialises in rice, with a wide variety of paella (including vegetarian and the traditional chicken-rabbit variety), black rice made with squid ink, "soupy rice" and fideua, which is like paella but with noodles. A few meat dishes, too.

The Paseo del Prado and the Retiro Park
Alfredo's Barbacoa
Calle Lagasca 5; https://alfredos-barbacoa.es; €
Alfredo's is one of the first good restaurants in Madrid for hamburgers – 40 years and going strong, now with a second restaurant a little north of Santiago Bernabéu soccer stadium.

El Brilliante
Plaza del Emperador Carlos V;
www.barelbrillante.es; €
Before or after the Reina Sofía museum, pop into this most typical of Madrid bars for a beer or two and their famous *bocadillo de calamares*, a long roll stuffed with fried squid rings, or tuck into the meatballs or grilled prawns.

Bumpgreen
Calle Velázquez 11; www.bumpgreen.com; €
Open-brick walls and a vertical garden set the scene at *Bumpgreen*, which specialises in organic produce and offers quinoa porridge for breakfast and a wide range of salads as well as fish and meat dishes, juices and cocktails.

El Perro y La Galleta
Calle Claudio Coello 1;
www.elperroylagalleta.com; €€
Dogs feature prominently in the décor at this smart bistro-style café by the park. A varied menu of modern Spanish dishes includes plenty of choices for vegetarians. It is good for breakfast too. Other locations around the city.

Vinoteca García de la Navarra
Calle Montalbán 3,
www.garciadelanavarra.com; €€
Pedro and Luis García de Navarra – chef and sommelier respectively – are the well-respected brothers behind this modern Spanish gastrobar and restaurant, which is so successful that they also opened *La Taberna del Pedro* next door. There is a wide selection of wines by the glass.

Plaza de Santa Ana, Barrio de las Letras and Lavapiés
Bodega de los Secretos
Calle San Blas 4;
https://bodegadelossecretos.com; €€
Hidden away on a quiet side street, the restaurant sprawls through a labyrinth of underground wine cellars dating back to the seventeenth century. Tables in romantic arched alcoves ensure privacy and there is a great menu of modern Spanish dishes.

Cebo
Hotel Urban, Carrera de San Jerónimo 34; www.cebomadrid.com/es; €€€€
After working with Ferran and Albert Adrià, Aurelio Morales opened his own restaurant in 2016. Dazzling dishes might include tiny shrimp emerging from a spray of zingy citrus foam. New Michelin star in 2024.

Chuka Ramen Bar
Calle Echegaray 9; www.chukaramenbar.com; €
Chuka mixes Japanese and Chinese cuisines to create an original menu that features bowls of tasty ramen noodles as well as gyozas and bao buns. Always packed so book ahead.

La Fisna
Calle Amparo 91; www.instagram.com/lafisna.vinoycata/?hl=es; €
A traditional bodega has been given a new lease of life after being taken over by wine lovers. There is a shop at the back, while the bar has a changing selection of at least forty wines by the glass and good cheese and charcuterie as well as more elaborate tapas.

El Lacón
Calle Manuel Fernández y González 8; www.mesonellacon.com; €

Superb presentation at Cebo

This very popular bar off Plaza de Santa Ana is a good place to start a tapas crawl. Order a beer or a glass of wine and you are given a complimentary tapa.

Moharaj
Calle Ave María 18; tel 91 5271787; €

There are quite a few Indian restaurants to choose from on this hill in Lavapiés, but in-the-know locals rate *Moharaj* most highly. Most of the food is prepared to order. Try the prawns rezala, matar paneer and the lamb rogan josh.

La Sanabresa
Calle Amor de Dios 12; tel: 91 429 0338; €

The *Sanabresa* is a mad whirl of packed tables and rushing waiters. Most people have one of the bargain set menus, starting perhaps with garlic mushrooms followed by meatballs, hake or spare ribs. They don't take bookings but the queue moves fast.

Taberna de Antonio Sánchez
Calle Mesón de Paredes 13;
www.tabernaantoniosanchez.com; €

Founded in 1830 by a matador, there is a bullfighting theme at this classic bar and restaurant, which has a zinc bar, marble tables, tiled walls and a bull's head on the wall. Have a draught vermouth, some tapas or a meal.

Taberna La Dolores
Plaza de Jesús 4; tel: 91 4292243; €

Pretty tavern with a tiled exterior that has been open for more than a century.

Known for its draught beer, so order a *caña* and a couple of *montaditos* – bread with tasty toppings.

Triciclo
Calle Santa Maria 28; www.eltriciclo.es; €€

The creative cuisine at *Triciclo* bar and restaurant is spiced up with a few fusion touches. It is very popular so book ahead and if it is full, try sister restaurant *Tándem* down the road at No. 39.

La Venencia
Calle Echegaray 7; www.lavenencia.com; €

One of the best-loved bars in Madrid, *La Venencia* is as stripped back as it gets, with just a wooden bar, barrels of sherry, faded posters on the walls and some tables at the back. Serving only several varieties of sherry and some basic tapas, it has been going since the 1930s and of course Hemingway was a regular.

Chueca, Malasaña and Conde Duque

Angelita
Calle Reina 4; www.madrid-angelita.es; €€

This gastrobar with lots of interesting wines by the glass has a daily-changing menu of dishes made with the best seasonal produce. The cocktail bar gets lively after midnight.

Bodega de la Ardosa
Calle Colón 13; www.laardosa.es; €

With its red paintwork and smoked glass sign, this is a truly *madrileño* place. You either sit on stools around

Taberna La Dolores is known for its selection of draft beers

Café Moderno

barrels or dive under the bar to one of the secret tables at the back. The freshly-made tortilla is legendary, made to the recipe of the owner's mother.

Bolívar
Calle Manuela Malasaña 28;
www.restaurantebolivar.com; €€
Excellent produce coupled with a creative touch and slick service have made this small restaurant a word-of-mouth success. Inside it is all subtle stylishness with a menu of creative classics, such as the sirloin with foie in a Port reduction.

Café Comercial
Glorieta de Bilbao 7;
http://cafecomercialmadrid.com; €
One of Madrid's greatest traditional cafés, opened since 1887 and revamped

in 2017. Fortunately, the atmosphere has survived, and it is still a favourite haunt of writers, actors and artists.

Café Moderno
Plaza de Comendadoras 1; tel: 604 54 52 51; €
In this updated classic café, you can have pizzas, international tapas and more, in a venue used by Pedro Almodóvar for his film *Parallel Mothers*. There's a nice outdoor seating area on *Comendadoras*, one of the prettiest squares in central Madrid.

Celicioso
Calle Barquillo 19;
https://celicioso.shop/madrid; €
Following the success of their nearby bakery (calle Hortaleza 3), *Celicioso* opened a café in the *Only You Boutique Hotel*. There are gluten-free cakes, sandwiches, burgers and salads, as well as juices and smoothies, to eat in or take away.

El Cisne Azul
Calle Gravina 27; www.elcisneazul.com; €€
A tapa bar most famous for its mushrooms of different kinds, they also have other things, including several unusual vegetarian options. Their first, smaller location is at Gravina 19; both places usually crowded.

La Dichosa
Calle Bernardo López García 11;
http://ladichosa.es; €
With its blue, black and white décor and arty clientele, this gastrobar in

Tortilla and wine at Bodega de la Ardosa

Madrid-style tripe at Café Gijón.

Lorca and Neruda were once regulars at this pretty tiled restaurant in trendy Chueca, which opened in 1854. Now, it has a modern Spanish menu using a lot of organic produce. You can eat all day and it is handy for breakfast or coffee and cake in the afternoon too.

Plaza de España and Moncloa
Bar Casa Paco
Calle Altamirano 38; tel: 91 5432821; €
This busy bar is open from breakfast time onwards and offers a good-value set lunch, but most people come for a wedge of one of their tortilla omelettes, which are stacked up along the counter for you to choose from.

the bohemian Conde Duque area brings a bit of New York sassiness to Madrid. Check out the blackboards for unusual wines by the glass or try one of the draught artisan beers.

La Casa de Valencia
Paseo del Pintor Rosales 58;
www.lacasavalencia.es; €€
Founded in 1975 opposite the Oeste park, the *Casa de Valencia* is the place to come for an authentic Valencian paella or other rice dish – with lobster, monkfish or vegetables perhaps. Order some shellfish or a salad to start and allow a couple of hours to enjoy your lunch.

La Manduca de Azagra
Calle Sagasta 14;
https://lamanducadeazagra.com; €€€
Much of the produce at this well-designed restaurant comes from the owner's village in Navarra, a region renowned for its vegetables as well as its elegant cuisine and wines. Try the cristal peppers. Popular with media people, this is a smart place with superb food.

Cuenllas
Calle Ferraz 3; www.cuenllas.es; €€
Cuenllas started out as a delicatessen in 1939 and fifty years later added a tapas bar and restaurant with excellent service. It is all about the quality of the produce here. The crab cannelloni and the *callos a la madrileña* are favourites.

Taberna La Carmencita
Calle Libertad 16; www.tabernalacarmencita.es; €

Bar Casa Paco at night

Punto Vegano
Calle Luisa Fernanda 27; tel: 91 2940840; €

Run by a young Uruguayan couple,
this vegan café near the Templo
de Debod serves tasty hot dishes,
including homemade ravioli and
quinoa burgers, as well as sandwiches,
salads, cakes and juices.

La Sifonería
Calle Martín de los Heros 27;
www.lasifoneria.com; €

Run by two brothers, this popular
bar and restaurant is decorated with
vintage soda siphons and has good
Spanish and international dishes to
share as well as a fixed-price lunch.
The bar offers draught vermouth,
wines by the glass and cocktails.

Paseo de la Castellana and Salamanca

Café Gijón
Paseo de Recoletos 21; www.cafegijon.com; €

With red velvet banquettes and
marble tables, the *Gijón*, which
opened in 1888, is one of the few
traditional cafés left in the city and
is a key element of the city's literary
heritage. As well as drinks and
snacks, there is a fixed-price lunch.

DiverXO
Hotel NH Collection Eurobuilding, calle Padre
Damián 23; http://diverxo.com; €€€€

Dabiz Muñoz is the only chef in Madrid
to have been awarded three Michelin
stars. Eating at *DiverXO* is an astounding

experience, with spectacular Asian-
inspired food and a theatrical vibe.
You need to book months ahead.

Gourmet Experience Serrano
El Corte Inglés; calle Serrano 52;
www.elcorteingles.es/help/en/centres-
and-companies/gourmet-experience; €€

Eat food by Michelin-starred chefs at
more affordable prices in this gourmet
food court on the top floor of El Corte
Inglés department store. Try *StreetXo* –
a simpler version of *DiverXO* – or the
Mexican cuisine at *Cascabel*. There is
gourmet ice cream by the Roca brothers
at *Rocambolesc* too. Another *Gourmet
Experience* is based at El Corte Inglés
just north of Nuevos Ministerios.

Ramon Freixa Madrid
Hotel Único, calle Claudio Coello 67;
www.ramonfreixamadrid.com; €€€€

Catalan chef Ramon Freixa has two
Michelin stars at his glamorous
restaurant, where the seasonally-changing
menu might include Galician beef rib
with mortadella and sea urchin. This is
a great choice for a special occasion.

Sacha
Calle Juan Hurtado de Mendoza 11;
www.restaurantesacha.com; €€€

Consistently rated as one of the best
restaurants in the city, *Sacha* was founded
more than forty years ago by the parents
of the current owner and is renowned for
both its superb modern Spanish cuisine
and the warm, unstuffy atmosphere.

Michelin-star quality at Ramon Freixa Madrid

Nightlife

Madrid is one of the liveliest cities in Europe after the sun goes down. With first-class cultural venues as well as bars and clubs to suit all tastes, you will never be stuck for something to do in the evening. The places recommended here are just a small selection of what is on offer, whether you want to see a flamenco show, go to a concert or dance the night away.

Opera, zarzuela and classical music

Auditorio Nacional de Música
Calle Príncipe de Vergara 146;
www.auditorionacional.mcu.es
The home of the National Orchestra and Choir of Spain, with two main halls and smaller spaces. There are several concerts every day by Spanish and international orchestras and individual musicians.

Teatro Real
Plaza de Isabel II; www.teatroreal.es/en
Madrid's opera house is one of the most prestigious in the world, with a programme of events from Sept–June. It is also a leading venue for classical music concerts and dance performances.

Teatro de la Zarzuela
Calle Jovellanos 4; tel: 91 5245400;
http://teatrodelazarzuela.mcu.es
This charming nineteenth-century theatre is the home of zarzuela, the Madrid version of light opera, which is a mixture of a play and a musical, with a lot of humour thrown in. Most popular in the nineteenth century, the form is undergoing a bit of a revival.

Live music

Clamores
Calle Alburquerque 14; tel: 91 4455480;
www.salaclamores.es
Clamores specialises in jazz and blues but you might also hear flamenco, folk or tango. It's a popular place – all sorts of artists and bands, from Spain and all over the world, perform at this atmospheric basement club in the Chamberí neighbourhood.

Sala La Riviera
Paseo Bajo de la Vírgen del Puerto; tel: 91 3652415; http://salariviera.com
Down by the Manzanares River, *La Riviera* is a landmark venue in Madrid. With two indoor spaces, a circular dance floor and a terrace, it is a late-night club as well as a place to see well-known international musicians.

WiZink Center
Avenida Felipe II; tel: 91 4449949;
www.wizinkcenter.es
This large venue in the Salamanca disrrict, which most people still refer to using its original name – the Palacio de Deportes – hosts an eclectic array of music and sporting events.

Performance at the Teatro de la Zarzuela

Flamenco
Cardamomo
Calle Echegaray 15; www.cardamomo.es

Just about all the best contemporary flamenco musicians and dancers have appeared at this popular venue, including Estrella Morente and Antonio Carmona. There are usually three performances every evening, with various options for food and drinks.

Tablao Flamenco 1911 (old name Villa Rosa)
Plaza Santa Ana 15, (tile facade); https://tablaoflamenco1911.com/en/

Considered the oldest continuously operating flamenco *tablao*, this venue has lovely decoration inside and out, and is suitably intimate for this kind of show. Three or four daily shows, one hour long.

Film
Cine Doré – Filmoteca Española
Calle Santa Isabel 3; www.cultura.gob.es/cultura/areas/cine/mc/fe/cine-dore/programacion.html

This Art Nouveau cinema was one of the first in Madrid and now houses the Filmoteca Española (Spanish Film Institute). As well as the programme of classic and avant-garde films, talks and other events, it has a café, bookshop and roof terrace.

Golem
Calle Martín de los Heros 14; www.golem.es/golem/golem-madrid

There are several cinemas showing films in the original versions on and around calle Martín de los Heros, just off Plaza de España. Golem usually has at least six to choose from and has reduced prices on Mondays and Wednesdays, as well as Sunday evenings.

Bars and clubs
1862 Dry Bar
Calle Pez 27; www.instagram.com/1862drybar/?hl=es

Run by top barman Alberto Martínez, this is a place for classic cocktails. Housed in a mid-nineteenth-century palatial, it is a good spot for a drink before or after dinner.

Florida Park
Retiro Park; https://floridapark.es/en/florida-nights

As well as a café-restaurant by day, this venue is a classic nightclub, hosting impressive shows and renowned DJs.

Marula Café
Calle Caños Viejos 3; www.marulacafe.com

The funky soul vibe goes on till dawn at this club near Plaza de la Paja. There are different DJs every night and often there is a live band too.

Museo Chicote
Gran Vía 12; www.museochicote.com

This legendary cocktail bar has been attracting famous customers since the 1930s, including Ernest Hemingway, Salvador Dalí, Grace Kelly and Ava Gardner. While *Museo Chicote* now has more of a club vibe, the original Art Deco interior survives and it makes for an atmospheric drink.

Facade of the ornate Villa Rosa restaurant

Essentials

Accessible travel

Madrid has improved its facilities for travellers with disabilities but there is still a long way to go. Most hotels have at least one adapted room, but it is worth checking the specifics beforehand. Most museums and sights are wheelchair accessible. All buses and 60 percent of the metro system are accessible. The Madrid tourist board website provides comprehensive information for visitors with disabilities with a downloadable booklet (www.es madrid.com/en/accessible-madrid).

Age restrictions

The age of consent and the minimum age for marriage in Spain is 16. You must be 18 to drive a car and 21 to hire a vehicle. The legal age for buying and drinking alcohol is 18.

Budgeting

While not a cheap city, spending a few days in Madrid is not as expensive as other major European capitals.

Prices for food and drink do of course vary a lot from basic bars to smart places, but a small beer usually costs between €1.30 and €2. A glass of wine is normally from €1.80 to €4. Expect to pay around €1.50–2.50 for a coffee. A main course at an economic restaurant is around €12, while at a mid-range place – which is the norm in Madrid – €15–23 is normal. At a high-end restaurant, the price goes up to €25–40.

A room in a basic but adequate hotel costs around €60–80. Mid-range hotels tend to charge between €80 and €150. Deluxe hotels sometimes have surprisingly reasonable rates, starting from €150 and in most places the price does not exceed €350.

A taxi from the airport to the city centre costs €35, which is a flat rate, and the airport-Atocha bus costs €5. A single bus journey costs €1.50. The metro costs €1.50 for up to five stops and up to €2 for more than five stops. The useful 10-ride metrobus ticket costs €12.20 and is valid on the metro and bus though not from the airport. Ask about deals at bigger metro stops; recent years have seen lower rates. The Madrid Tourist Travel Pass, available from metro stations, includes metro, bus and local trains and is available for one to seven days, starting at €10.00 for one day (includes airport supplement).

The Paseo del Arte ticket (€32.00) allows admission to the Prado, Reina Sofía and Thyssen-Bornemisza museums and represents a saving of 20 percent compared to individual entrance tickets. It is available from the museums and their websites. The

Palm trees in Atocha Station

Five Museums: Another Madrid pass (€12) includes the Sorolla, Cerralbo, Lázaro Galdiano, Romanticism and Decorative Arts museums and is valid for 10 days. The Annual Membership Card for National Museums includes many of the Madrid museums (though not the Thyssen) as well as some museums in Toledo or other cities (€36.60). Find a list of museums included on this card here: www.museoreinasofia. es/en/visit/opening-hours-and-ticket-prices/annual-membership.

Children

Spanish people adore children and they are made welcome just about everywhere, even in smart restaurants. Most hotels allow children under 12 to stay at no extra charge in existing beds. Cots are usually provided on request and babysitting can be arranged. Children can travel free on public transport up to the age of four.

Clothing

While *madrileños* tend to be smartly dressed, it is fine to wear shorts around the city in warm weather, even in the evening, except for high-end restaurants. Ties are required for men in very few places. Informal clothes are usually okay for visiting churches, but women might want to take a scarf. In winter, take a hat and gloves as it can be very cold. In spring and autumn, you usually only need a light jacket.

Crime and safety

Madrid is generally a safe city but petty crime is all too common. Try to keep important documents and valuables on your person rather than in a bag and only take what is absolutely necessary out with you. Be particularly vigilant on the metro (especially when travelling to and from the airport), at the Rastro street market and in busy areas such as the Puerta del Sol and the Gran Vía. At pavement cafés, keep bags on your lap with the strap around your wrist.

Customs

Travellers from EU countries may take unlimited goods for personal use into and out of Spain. This amount is regarded as up to 800 cigarettes, 10 litres of spirits and 90 litres of wine. Visitors may bring up to €10,000 into or out of the country without declaring it.

Tourists from outside EU countries can claim back IVA (value added tax) on purchases made in stores that participate in the tax-free shopping scheme (ask for a tax-free form and get it stamped by customs upon departure – goods must be taken out of the EU within three months of the purchase date). The minimum purchase amount is now €0.01.

Electricity

The electrical current is 220 volts. There is no problem using 240-volt UK appliances. Sockets take round, two-pin plugs.

Metro sign

110

DIRECTORY ESSENTIALS

Embassies and consulates

Many countries have embassies in Madrid, including the following:

Australia: Torre Emperador, Paseo de la Castellana 259d, 24th floor, tel: 91 3536600; www.spain.embassy.gov.au.

Canada: Torre Emperador, Paseo de la Castellana 259d, tel: 91 3828400; www.international.gc.ca/country-pays/spain-espagne/madrid.aspx?lang=eng.

Ireland: Paseo de la Castellana 46, 4; tel: 91 4364093; www.ireland.ie/en/spain/madrid/.

UK: Torre Emperador, Paseo de la Castellana 259d; tel: 91 714 6400; www.gov.uk/world/spain.

United States: Calle de Serrano 75; tel: 91 5872200; https://es.usembassy.gov/.

Emergencies

The Foreign Tourist Assistance Service, based at the police station (*comisaría de policía*) at calle Leganitos 19 (tel: 91 3224097), has multilingual staff to help tourists report crime and provide support with contacting family, banks etc. If you lose your passport, report it to the police and contact the relevant consulate or embassy to obtain an emergency document to enable you to travel. See also the Health section below.

Emergency services: dial 112 for police, ambulance and fire services. Multilingual operators are available.

Etiquette

If you are introduced to people by friends, it is usual to kiss lightly on both cheeks, though this has become less frequent since COVID. If you are invited to someone's home, try to take a small gift, such as chocolates. It is normal to greet people in a lift. Spaniards do not usually share tables in bars and restaurants, even in fast-food and busy places.

Festivals

Carnaval. February–March. Celebrating the end of Lent, carnival involves processions, music, theatre, activities for children and fancy-dress parties. The most prestigious event is the spectacular masked ball at the Círculo de Bellas Artes.

Semana Santa. March–April. The processions during Easter week in Madrid are not as lavish as in other cities, but are still worth seeing – with the advantage that you do not have to fight your way through crowds.

Dos de Mayo. Early May. The Dos de Mayo festival, which lasts for at least a week, commemorates Madrid's battle against French troops on May 2, 1808 with a lively programme of arts events, pop concerts and street festivals, focused in the Malasaña area. May 2 is also the Day of the Madrid Region (www.madrid.org/fiestasdel2demayo).

San Isidro. May 15 is the feast day of San Isidro, the patron saint of Madrid, which is celebrated with much merriment in the streets of the most traditional areas and in the Pradera de San Isidro park. There are bullfights,

San Isidro festival is held on 15th May

concerts and other events on for at least two weeks around the main date (www.esmadrid.com/en/san-isidro).

Feria del Libro. Late May–early June. During the Madrid Book Fair around 200 bookshops have stalls in the Retiro Park. There are signings and talks by dozens of leading Spanish and international authors and it is as much a social as a literary event (https://ferialibromadrid.com).

Suma Flamenca. June. Throughout June, there are performances by leading flamenco artists at large and small venues all over the city at this festival which is organised by the Madrid regional government (www.madrid.org/sumaflamenca).

PhotoEspaña. June–August. PhotoEspaña is a major festival of photography and visual arts that takes place in cultural venues and outdoor locations across the city, with exhibitions, talks by leading photographers, courses, workshops, guided visits and a wealth of other activities (www.phe.es).

Los Veranos de la Villa. July–August. Throughout the summer, classical, rock and jazz concerts as well as theatrical and dance performances are staged at indoor and outdoor venues across the city, including the Sabatini gardens and the Casa de Campo Park. There are also several outdoor cinema venues (www.veranosdelavilla.com).

Madrid Pride. Late June–early July. Madrid hosts one of the biggest and most riotous Pride festivals in the world. Attracting thousands of people, this is one of the busiest times of the year in the city with street parties, concerts and parades (http://madridorgullo.com).

San Cayetano, San Lorenzo and La Paloma. August 1–16. Madrid's most traditional street festivals, put on for locals rather than tourists, involve dressing up in traditional costume, dancing to live bands, alfresco eating and activities for all ages. Events take place along the sloping streets of the Austrias and Lavapiés neighbourhoods, the oldest and most characterful areas of the city (www.esmadrid.com/en/august-fiestas-madrid).

Health

The public health service is excellent and medical professionals usually speak good English. EU citizens are entitled to basic free medical treatment with the EHIC European Healthcard (www.ehic.org.uk) while UK nationals can access healthcare services in EEA countries via the Global Health Insurance Card (GHIC). Take photocopies of the card and your passport as you will need to present both at a clinic or hospital. It is strongly advisable to take out private health insurance, whether you have the EHIC/GHIC card or not.

If you have a medical emergency and need to go to hospital, the most central is the Hospital Clínico San Carlos in Moncloa (calle Profesor Martín Lagos; tel: 91 3303000). Look for the *Urgencias*

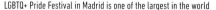
LGBTQ+ Pride Festival in Madrid is one of the largest in the world

(Accident and Emergency) department.

Pharmacists are thoroughly trained and can prescribe some medication though not antibiotics. Pharmacies are marked by a green neon cross and one in every district remains open all night and on holidays. The location and phone number of this *farmacia de guardia* is posted on the door of all the other pharmacies. All-night pharmacies can also be contacted by calling 098.

If you take prescription medication, ensure that you take extra supplies with you as Spanish chemists cannot accept foreign prescriptions. Given the dry climate and sun levels, it is a good idea to wear sunscreen and carry water with you in both summer and winter.

Tap water (*agua del grifo*) is excellent quality in Madrid and tastes fine. Although locals often drink bottled water, it is perfectly acceptable to ask for a glass or jug in bars and restaurants, even in smart places.

Hours and holidays

Business hours vary a lot in Madrid, but many offices operate from 9am until 5pm or 6pm. It is becoming less common to have a long break for lunch but it is always advisable to try and get anything important done before 2pm. Most banks are open Monday to Friday from 8.30am to 2.30pm. Some branches also open on Saturday mornings. Most shops in the centre are open from 9.30am to 8.30pm, including on Sundays. Small shops outside the

central area still close for lunch from 2pm until 5pm and often close on Saturday afternoons as well as all day on Sunday. Quite a few restaurants close on Sundays or Mondays.

Public holidays

January 1 *Año Nuevo*, New Year's Day
January 6 *Día de Reyes*, Epiphany
March 19 *San José*, St Joseph's Day (also Father's Day); not always a holiday in Madrid city.
May 1 *Fiesta de Trabajo*, Labour Day
May 2 *Día de la Comunidad de Madrid*, Day of the Madrid Region
May 15 *San Isidro* (patron saint of Madrid)
August 15 *Asunción de la Vírgen*, Assumption of the Virgin Mary
October 12 *Día Nacional de España*, National Day of Spain, Columbus Day
November 1 *Todos los Santos*, All Saints' Day
November 9 *Nuestra Señora de la Almudena*, Our Lady of the Almudena (patron of Madrid)
December 6 *Día de la Constitución Española*, Constitution Day
December 8 *Día de la Inmaculada Concepción*, Immaculate Conception Day
December 25 *Navidad,* Christmas Day
Movable dates: During Easter, between late March and mid-April, Maundy Thursday, Good Friday and Easter Sunday are public holidays. Easter Monday is a normal working day in Madrid, though treated as a holiday

Lunchtime at the Mercado San Miguel

in some other parts of Spain.

LGBTQ+ travellers

Madrid has one of the liveliest LGBTQ+ scenes in Europe. The narrow streets of the Chueca neighbourhood are lined with bars, clubs and shops. This is also the hub of Madrid Pride festival – see Festivals above.

Media

Print media

The main national newspapers are *El País*, *El Mundo*, *ABC* and *La Vanguardia*. *El País* has an online English edition. All issue weekly cultural and entertainment listings' supplements, usually on Fridays.

Money

Currency

The currency of Spain is the euro (€), which is made up of 100 cents. There are notes in denominations of 5, 10, 20, 50, 100 and 200. There are coins to a value of €1 and €2, as well as 50, 20, 10, five, two and one cents. It can be very hard to use 100- and 200-euro notes, sometimes even 50 euros if purchase amount is small.

Credit cards

Cards are widely used and contactless payments are standard. It is normal to use cash for small amounts in bars and shops.

Cash machines

There are machines at banks all over the city, with instructions in English and other languages. Try to avoid taking out cash at night from a machine in the street for safety reasons. Most banks also have machines inside and there are cash dispensers in El Corte Inglés department stores. There are two main systems, Euro 6000 and Servired, so if you have trouble with a machine, look for a cashpoint that uses the other system.

Traveller's cheques

These are not widely used but can be cashed at banks, Bureaux de Change and major hotels. While you can use them in stores in tourist areas, traveller's cheques are not usually accepted in shops. In addition to being more difficult to cash, the exchange rate or commission is often worse than at a cashpoint.

Tipping

There is no culture of leaving hefty tips in Spain. At high-end restaurants, leave 10 percent, but at most places around 5 percent is fine. It is typical but by no means compulsory to leave small change when paying for coffees, drinks or a taxi. At luxury hotels, however, international customs prevail.

Taxes

The standard rate of Value Added Tax (Impuesto de Valor Añadido, IVA) is 21 percent, but a reduced rate of

A well-stocked street kiosk

10 percent applies for hotel stays, bars, restaurants, cultural institutions and entertainment venues, including cinemas and theatres. It is usually – but not always – included in stated prices.

Post

Spain has a nationalised postal system, called Correos. There are surprisingly few post offices (*oficina de correos*) in Madrid, although stamps (*sellos*) are available at tobacconists (*estancos*). The main post office is on Plaza de Cibeles (Paseo del Prado 1) and there are post offices in El Corte Inglés department stores. Postboxes are yellow. A postcard or letter costs €1.70 to Europe and €2.10 to the US.

Religion

Roman Catholicism is the national religion in Spain and nearly 70 percent of citizens identify as such. St George's English Church (calle Nuñez de Balboa 43, www.stgeorgesmadrid.org), part of the Church of England, is a diverse Christian community and holds services on Sundays. People of Muslim faith can worship at the mosque at the Centro Cultural Islámico de Madrid (calle Salvador de Madariaga 4; https://centro-islamico.com). The Beth Yaacov synagogue is at calle Balmes 3.

Smoking

Smoking is not allowed in bars, restaurants, shops or other indoor public places or on public transport. Most hotels only allow smoking in designated rooms and many ban it altogether.

Telephones

The country code for Spain is 34. The local code for Madrid is 91 and this prefix must be dialled when you are in the city. To make an international call, dial 00 followed by the relevant country code. There are public phone boxes but it is often easier and cheaper to make international calls from a *locutorio* shop, where you can also buy phone cards. The main mobile operators are Movistar, Vodafone and Orange, with shops all over the centre. You can buy a pay-as-you-go phone or just a Spanish SIM card to use during your stay. As of 2017, roaming charges for customers within the EU were abolished but because of Brexit, UK mobile operators are no longer required to offer free data roaming to UK customers in the EU. Check with your provider for current policies.

Time zones

Spain is on Central European Time, which is one hour ahead of Greenwich Mean Time and British Summer Time. It is six hours ahead of New York.

Toilets

There are public toilets at some central points, but they are a bit thin on the ground. Most bars will not mind if you go in to use the facilities, but it is courteous to buy a coffee or a

Madrid Barajas airport

bottle of water. You can also pop into large hotels or museums, which usually have toilets in the lobby area. The Corte Inglés department store is another option, as well as bus stations in Moncloa and Plaza de Castilla. Look for an S (Señoras) or M (Mujeres) sign on the door for ladies' toilets and C (Caballeros) or H (Hombres) for the men's.

Tourist information

The Madrid tourism organisation (www.esmadrid.com/en) has comprehensive practical and background information on its website. You can also consult the useful websites of the Madrid Region (www.turismomadrid. es) and the Spanish tourist office (www.spain.info) to plan your trip.

The main tourist office is at Plaza Mayor 27. It has multilingual staff and is open every day of the year from 9.30am to 9.30pm. There are tourist information kiosks at key points around the city centre and at Terminal 2 and Terminal 4 at the airport.

Tours and guides

You might enjoy embarking on an organised tapas tour when you arrive, so that you know how and what to order for the rest of your stay. Devour Madrid (https://madridfoodtour. com) has a range of options and knowledgeable, entertaining guides. Madrid and Beyond (www.madridand beyond.com) can organise all sorts of private specialist tours in the city and throughout Spain. Rough Guides offer a range of exciting and unique tailor-made trips in Madrid and beyond devised by local experts to your specifications (www.roughguides.com).

Transport

Arrival by air
Adolfo Suárez Madrid-Barajas airport (www.aena.es/en/adolfo-suarez-madrid-barajas.html) is 12km (7.5 miles) east of the city centre. There are three terminals in the original section plus the newer, separate Terminal 4, which handles Iberia and British Airways flights. A free shuttle connects Terminal 4 with the rest of the airport. Easyjet and Ryanair use Terminal 1.

There is a fixed €35 taxi fare to anywhere in the centre and the journey takes 20–30 minutes. The metro from the airport costs €1.50–2 plus a €3 supplement. You need to change lines at Nuevos Ministerios station to get to the centre, which is easy enough but obviously only advisable with manageable luggage.

The 24-hour Airport Express bus service (number 203), with luggage racks, costs €5 and takes 20–40 minutes, with stops at Plaza de Cibeles and Atocha station (www.emtmadrid. es/Aeropuerto). Route 200 on the municipal bus network goes from the airport to the Avenida de América transport hub and costs €1.50.

The ceiling mosaic at the Almudena Cathedral

The C-1 local train (look for *Cercanías* signs) runs from Terminal 4 to the centre, stopping at Valdebebas, Fuente de la Mora, Chamartin, Nuevos Ministerios, Recoletos and Atocha station, and costs €2.60 single.

Public transport

Madrid has an efficient public transport system with extensive, easy to use metro and bus networks (www.crtm.es). See Budgeting above for fares and ticket information.

Metro

The metro system operates from 6am until 1.30am. There are 12 lines, covering the whole city. See www.esmadrid.com/en/madrid-metro and www.metromadrid.es/en for further information.

Bus

Buses run from 6am to 11.30pm. There is also an extensive night bus network through the nocturnal hours, which are known as *búhos* (owls) and leave from Plaza de Cibeles. You can buy a ticket from the driver or, if you have a 10-ride Metrobus ticket, punch it in the machine at the front of the bus.

Useful routes include No. 2, which goes through Plaza de España, Gran Vía and Plaza de Cibeles to the Retiro Park, and No. 3, which goes along the calle Bailen, Plaza de España, Gran Vía and up calle Hortaleza, between the Chueca and Malasaña neighbourhoods.

There are also two routes with ten-seat electric buses that wiggle around the narrow streets of the centre. The M1 leaves from Plaza Canalejas near calle Alcalá at Sevilla metro station and heads south to La Latina, Tirso de Molina and Lavapiés, Madrid's most traditional areas. The M3 goes southwest from Sevilla, behind Plaza Mayor to La Latina area and ends at Puerta de Toledo. Two "zero" lines are completely free: 001 (Atocha – Moncloa, along Gran Vía and Princesa) and 002 (Puerta de Toledo – Argüelles, through Malasaña) See www.esmadrid.com/en/getting-around-madrid-by-bus and www.emtmadrid.es/Home for more information.

Trains

The Cercanías rail network covers the Madrid region and is useful for day trips to El Escorial, Aranjuez and Alcalá de Henares (www.esmadrid.com/en/madrid-cercanias-train). For train travel around Spain, see www.renfe.com. The main stations are Chamartín (renamed Clara Campoamor in 2023) in the north and Atocha (now called Almudena Grandes) in the south, with two underground rail links between the two: some trains run through Sol and others run through Recoletos.

Taxis

Taxis are white with a red diagonal stripe on the sides and are plentiful and not too expensive – a short hop costs €5–10. A green light on the roof

Traffic on Gran Vía

and a "Libre" sign shows the vehicle is available. You can call a cab from Radio-Taxi (tel: 91 447 3232) or Teletaxi (tel: 91 371 2131; www.tele-taxi.es). Uber also operates in Madrid and rides can be booked through the app (www.uber.com/es/en/?uclick_id=1ce90bd5-4aae-4cec-a2ca-c28beecbea9e).

Driving

There is no need to drive around central Madrid and parking can be difficult. Most sights are within walking distance or a few stops away by bus or metro. The minimum driving age is 18, seatbelts are compulsory and there are strict drink driving laws – the limit is 50mg of alcohol per 100ml of blood and just 25mg for drivers who have held a licence for less than two years. Driving is on the right.

Car hire

You may want to hire a car to do some day trips. Rates are generally reasonable and bookings usually require a credit card. Be aware that the rental company might reserve a hefty deposit on your card. While the payment is not actually taken, you need to have sufficient credit available. The minimum age for renting a car is 21. A national driver's licence is fine for EU citizens and usually for US citizens, but always check the conditions. Major companies have offices at the airport and train stations. Try Sixt (www.sixt.co.uk/car-hire/spain), Avis (www.avis.es) or Europcar (www.europcar.es/Madrid). Spanish companies National Atesa-Enterprise (www.enterprise.es/es/atesa.html) and Pepe Car (www.pepecar.com) may be cheaper.

Visas and passports

Visitors from countries that are part of the Schengen Agreement can enter Spain without passport control at borders, but everyone is legally required to carry a valid passport or national identity card while in the country. Identification is often required at hotels and other places.

For non-Schengen countries, EU nationals can enter Spain with either a passport or a valid national ID card. Non-EU nationals generally need a passport to enter Spain, and a visa may be required unless your country has a visa waiver agreement with Spain. From 2024, travellers from visa-exempt countries outside the EU will also need to apply for an ETIAS (European Travel Information and Authorization System) before entering Spain (due to be operational in early 2025).

Weights and measures

Spain uses the metric system.

Women travellers

Women travelling alone should generally not encounter problems in Madrid and it is perfectly normal to eat on your own. However, it is important to take standard precautions as in any major city.

The metro is a great way to get around the city

Language

It is very useful and rewarding to learn some basic phrases in Spanish. English is widely spoken in shops and restaurants in tourist areas and in hotels and major museums, but is certainly not understood everywhere, particularly among older people.

As a general rule, the accent falls on the second-to-last syllable, unless it is otherwise marked with an accent (´) or the word ends in D, L, R or Z, when the accent is on the last syllable.

Vowels in Spanish are always pronounced the same way. The double L (LL) is pronounced like the y in 'yes', the double R is rolled. The H is silent in Spanish, whereas J (and G when it precedes an E or I) is pronounced like a guttural H (similar to the end sound of Scottish *loch*).

When addressing someone you are not familiar with, use the more formal 'usted'. The informal 'tú' is reserved for relatives and friends.

Basic words and phrases

yes *sí*
no *no*
thank you (very much) *(muchas) gracias*
you're welcome *de nada*
okay *bien/vale*
please *por favor*
excuse me *perdóneme/perdón*
Can you help me? *¿Me puede ayudar?*

Do you speak English? (formal) *¿Habla inglés?*
Please speak more slowly *Hable más despacio, por favor*
I don't understand *No entiendo*
I'm sorry *Lo siento/Perdone*
I don't know *No lo sé*
No problem *No hay problema*
Where is...? *¿Dónde está...?*
I am looking for... *Estoy buscando*
That's it *Ese es*
Let's go *Vámonos*
At what time? *¿A qué hora?*
When? *¿Cuándo?*
here *aquí*
there *allí*

Greetings

Hello!/Hi! *¡Hola!* or *Buenos días*
How are you? (formal/informal) *¿Cómo está?/¿Qué tal?*
What is your name? (formal) *¿Cómo se llama usted?*
Fine thanks *Muy bien, gracias*
My name is... *Me llamo...*
Mr/Miss/Mrs *Señor/Señorita/Señora*
Pleased to meet you *¡Encantado(a)!*
I am British/American *Soy británico/norteamericano*
See you tomorrow *Hasta mañana*
See you soon *Hasta pronto/hasta luego*
Have a good day *Que tenga un buen día*
goodbye *adiós*
good afternoon/evening *buenas tardes*
good night *buenas noches*

Helpful signs

On arrival

airport *aeropuerto*
customs *aduana*
train station *estación de tren*
platform *andén*
ticket *billete*
bus *autobús*
bus stop *parada de autobús*
metro station *estación de metro*
toilets *servicios/aseos/WC/baño*
taxi *taxi*

In the hotel

I'd like a (single/double) room *Quiero una habitación (individual/doble)*
... with bath *con baño*
... with a view *con vista*
Does that include breakfast? *¿Incluye desayuno?*
lift/elevator *ascensor*
air conditioning *aire acondicionado*

Numbers

1 *uno*
2 *dos*
3 *tres*
4 *cuatro*
5 *cinco*
6 *seis*
7 *siete*
8 *ocho*
9 *nueve*
10 *diez*
11 *once*
12 *doce*
13 *trece*
14 *catorce*
15 *quince*
16 *dieciseis*
17 *diecisiete*
18 *dieciocho*
19 *diecinueve*
20 *veinte*
100 *cien*
1,000 *mil*
10,000 *diez mil*
1,000,000 *un millón*

Days of the week

Monday *lunes*
Tuesday *martes*
Wednesday *miércoles*
Thursday *jueves*
Friday *viernes*
Saturday *sábado*
Sunday *domingo*

Seasons

Spring *primavera*
Summer *verano*
Autumn *otoño*
Winter *invierno*

Months

January *enero*
February *febrero*
March *marzo*
April *abril*
May *mayo*
June *junio*
July *julio*
August *agosto*
September *septiembre*
October *octubre*
November *noviembre*
December *diciembre*

Spoilt for choice

Books and film

From the books and plays of Golden Age writers to the films of Pedro Almodóvar, Madrid's literary and cinematic heritage is easily discoverable throughout the city. Around the Plaza de Santa Ana, you can see where Cervantes, Lope de Vega, Góngora, Moratín and other writers lived in the sixteenth, seventeenth and eighteenth centuries, which keeps their legacy very much alive. The Madrid of Benito Pérez Galdós, regarded as the Spanish Dickens or Balzac, is still recognisable around the Puerta del Sol too.

Pedro Almodóvar has showcased Madrid in most of his films, from the madness of the *movida madrileña* in *Labyrinth of Passions* in 1982 to the stylish modern city of *Julieta* in 2016. Other contemporary Spanish directors, such as Alejandro Amenábar, Álex de la Iglesia, Julio Medem, Cesc Gay and Jonás Trueba have depicted the city in very different and often alarming ways.

Books

Non-fiction

A Handbook for Travellers in Spain, by Richard Ford. Written in the mid-nineteenth century, this is still one of the best books about Spain, with a fascinating section on Madrid.

Everything is Happening, by Michael Jacobs. This short book explores the acclaimed author's lifelong fascination with Velázquez's masterpiece *Las Meninas* and clearly shows his affection for Madrid.

Madrid: A Cultural and Literary History, by Elizabeth Nash. A well-written, entertaining overview of how artists and writers lived and worked in the city over the centuries.

A Traveller's Companion to Madrid, by Hugh Thomas. This gives a good historical introduction, with excerpts from novels and journals including texts by George Borrow, V.S. Pritchett and Ernest Hemingway.

Ghosts of Spain, by Giles Tremlett. This account of travelling through Spain in the early twenty-first century is an invaluable preparation for visiting the city.

Hotel Florida: Truth, Love and Death in the Spanish Civil War, by Amanda Vaill. Fascinating telling of the lives of Ernest Hemingway, Martha Gellhorn Robert Capa and Arturo Barea during the Civil War at the *Hotel Florida*, which stood on the Gran Vía.

Fiction

The Forging of a Rebel, by Arturo Barea. Based on Barea's own life, this gives an insight into the turbulence in Madrid in the early twentieth century.

The Beehive, by Camilo José Cela. The classic novel by Nobel prize-

Spanish film stars Pedro Almodóvar, Penélope Cruz and Antonio Banderas

winner Cela is a vivid portrayal of life in Madrid in the 1940s.
Madrid Tales, edited by Helen Constantine. This collection of stories, translated by Margaret Jull Costa, is the perfect companion for a stay in the city. With pieces by Benito Pérez Galdós, Javier Marías and Elvira Lindo, amongst other leading Spanish authors.
The Time In Between (US version) and ***The Seamstress*** (UK version), by Maria Dueñas. Set partly in Madrid in the 1930s – 1940s and partly in Spanish Morocco, this is the story of a courageous young woman living a very interesting life in complicated times.
Fortunata and Jacinta, by Benito Pérez Galdós. One of the greatest works of Spanish literature, about life in Madrid in the late-nineteenth century. Several other novels by Galdós are also available in English,
Leaving the Atocha Station, by Ben Lerner. Published in 2011, this novel skewers the pretentiousness of foreigners in Madrid while also amusingly describing the city.
A Heart so White, by Javier Marías. Partly set in Madrid, this novel evokes an intriguing image of the city. Marías is widely regarded to be the greatest living Spanish writer.
Captain Alatriste, by Arturo Pérez Reverte. Seven historical fiction novels about a soldier of fortune in seventeenth century Spain, narrated by the soldier's young squire. Many of the novels are at least partly set in Madrid.

Winter in Madrid, by C.J. Sansom. This absorbing novel about a British spy gives a vivid picture of the desperate situation in Madrid after the Civil War.

Films

The Day of the Beast (1996). Alex de la Iglesia's anarchic comedy blazes a chaotic trail through Madrid in a search for the devil at Christmas.
The Flower of My Secret (1995). Almodóvar is at his best in this film, which captures the magic of Madrid and was shot in the Plaza Mayor and around Plaza de los Carros and Plaza de Callao.
Julieta (2016). Walk along calle Fernando VI and you will recognise the locations of some of the scenes from Almodóvar's mesmeric film.
Open your Eyes (1997). Worth seeing for the sight of a deserted Gran Vía alone, Alejandro Amenábar's film was remade as *Vanilla Sky* by Tom Cruise.
The Quince Tree Sun (1992). This documentary film by poetic filmmaker Víctor Erice follows the great artist Antonio López as he creates a painting.
Sex and Lucía (2001). Julio Medem's erotic film is set partly in Madrid and the main character lives in a traditional apartment on the Plaza de las Comendadoras.
Women on the Verge of a Nervous Breakdown (1988). Almodóvar's glorious romp through Madrid shows the city as its zaniest, with locations featuring the Jerónimos and Chamberí areas.

Don Quixote, Spain's most famous novel

About this book

The Rough Guides Walks & Tours series helps you discover the world's most exciting destinations through our expert-curated trip plans: a range of walks and tours designed to suit all budgets, interests and trip lengths. These walks, driving tours and site excursions cover the destination's most quintessential attractions as well as a range of lesser-known sights, while food and drink stops for refreshments en route are highlighted in boxes. If you're not sure which walk to pick, our Best walks & tours for... feature suggests which ones work best for particular interests. The introduction provides a destination overview, while the directory supports the walks and tours with all the essential information you need, as well as our pick of where to stay while you are there and select restaurant listings, to complement the more low-key options given in the trip plans.

About the author

Rough Guides Walks & Tours Madrid was updated by Anne Pinder, who has lived in Madrid for more years than in her native Iowa, USA. She has explored most of Spain on foot and by bicycle, including lesser-known rural destinations.

Perpetually curious, she loves talking to locals, learning new things and sharing her discoveries with other people. She writes an intermittent blog and newsletter (https://diverge.substack.com) as well as guiding cultural walks in Madrid and elsewhere.

Her work builds on content by Annie Bennett.

Help us update

We've gone to a lot of effort to ensure that this edition of the **Rough Guides Walks & Tours Madrid** is accurate and up-to-date. However, things change – places get "discovered", new gems open up, restaurants and rooms raise prices or lower standards. If you feel we've got it wrong or left something out, we'd like to know, and if you can remember the address, the website, whether or not it was free to enter – so much the better.

Please send your comments with the subject line "**Rough Guides Walks & Tours Madrid Update**" to mail@uk.roughguides.com. We'll acknowledge all contributions and send a copy of the next edition (or any other Rough Guide if you prefer) for the very best emails.

Credits

Rough Guides Walks & Tours Madrid
Editor: Libby Davies
Author: Anne Pinder
Picture Editor: Piotr Kala
Picture Manager: Tom Smyth
Cartography: Katie Bennett
Layout: Ankur Guha
Production Operations Manager: Katie Bennett
Publishing Technology Manager: Rebeka Davies
Head of Publishing: Sarah Clark
Photo credits: Alberto Espada/Grupo Andilana 100T;
Corrie Wingate/Apa Publications 6TL, 7MR, 12, 12/13B, 13R,
31, 38, 46L, 52/53, 54, 55R, 54/55, 79, 80, 80/81, 81R, 85,
86, 86/87, 87T, 87R, 98, 99, 109; Derby Hotels Collection
95, 101; iStock 4BL, 4MR, 4BR, 6BC, 11, 13T, 14/15, 18,
21T, 21B, 23, 32, 33, 37, 40/41, 43, 45, 48, 56, 57, 58/59,
68, 69R, 71, 82, 110, 111, 112, 113, 114, 115, 116, 117,
119; Leonardo 89, 90, 91, 96, 97, 105; Madrid Destino 70,
100, 103, 104T; Mandarin Oriental Hotel Group Limited
94; Meliá Hotels 92; Museo Thyssen-Bornemisza 46/47;
Palladium Hotel Group 93; Public domain 6MC, 24/25, 30,
50, 77R; Shutterstock 1, 4T, 6ML, 7MR, 7M, 7T, 8/9, 10, 16,
17R, 16/17, 19, 20, 22, 26/27, 28/29, 34, 35, 36, 39, 42, 44,
49, 51, 52L, 53, 60, 61, 62, 63, 64L, 64/65, 65, 66, 67, 68/69,
72, 73, 74, 75, 76, 76/77, 78, 83, 84, 100, 102, 103T, 104,
106, 107, 108, 118, 120, 121; Starwood Hotels & Resorts 47
Cover credits: Plaza Mayor **Shutterstock**

Printed in Czech Republic

This book was produced using **Typefi** automated
publishing software.

Distribution

UK, Ireland and Europe
Apa Publications (UK) Ltd
sales@roughguides.com
United States and Canada
Ingram Publisher Services
ips@ingramcontent.com
Australia and New Zealand
Booktopia
retailer@booktopia.com.au
Worldwide
Apa Publications (UK) Ltd
sales@roughguides.com

Special sales, content licensing and copublishing

Rough Guides can be purchased in bulk quantities
at discounted prices. We can create special editions,
personalised jackets and corporate imprints tailored to
your needs.
sales@roughguides.com
http://roughguides.com

Index

MAP LEGEND

- ● Start of tour
- → Tour & route direction
- ❶ Recommended sight
- ◎ Recommended restaurant/café
- ★ Place of interest
- ❶ Tourist information
- ✈ Airport

- ▭ Railway
- 🚌 Main bus station
- 🅿 Car park
- Ⓜ Metro station
- ✉ Main post office
- 1 Monument
- ✝ Church
- ✡ Synagogue

- Ⓜ Museum/gallery
- Theatre
- Castle
- Important building
- Park
- Urban area
- Non-urban area
- Transport hub

NOTES